DEATH
before
BIRTH

DEATH before BIRTH

Harold O. J. Brown

THOMAS NELSON PUBLISHERS

Nashville

Other books by Harold O. J. Brown:

Christianity and the Class Struggle
The Protest of a Troubled Protestant
Evangelium und Gewalt
The Reconstruction of the Republic: A Christian Theory of the State
  'Under God'

Third printing

Copyright © 1977 by Harold O. J. Brown

All rights reserved under International and Pan-American Conventions. Published in Nashville, Tennessee, by Thomas Nelson Inc., Publishers and simultaneously in Don Mills, Ontario, by Thomas Nelson & Sons (Canada) Limited. Manufactured in the United States of America.

Library of Congress Cataloging in Publication Data

Brown, Harold O J   1933-
   Death before birth.

   Includes bibliographical references.
   1. Abortion—United States.   2. Abortion—Religious aspects.   1. Title.
HQ767.5.U5B78   301   77-13884
ISBN 0-8407-5715-8 P.B.

*To all those robbed of the life which
they had not yet begun to enjoy, while
so many, in full knowledge of the facts,
do no more than bemoan an evil they could end.*

Contents

Oath of *Hippocrates*

"I swear by Apollo the physician, and Aesculapius, and Hygeia, and Panacea, and all the gods and goddesses that, according to my ability and judgment, I will keep this Oath and this stipulation —to reckon him who taught me this art equally dear to me as my parents, to share my substance with him, and relieve his necessities if required; to look upon his offspring in the same footing as my own brothers, and to teach them this art, if they shall wish to learn it, without fee or stipulation, and that by precept, lecture, and every other mode of instruction, I will impart a knowledge of the art to my own sons, and those of my teachers, and to disciples bound by a stipulation and oath according to the law of medicine, but to none others. I will follow that system of regimen which, according to my ability and judgment, I consider for the benefit of my patients, and abstain from whatever is deleterious and mischievous. I will give no deadly medicine to anyone if asked, nor suggest any such counsel; and in like manner I will not give to a woman a pessary to produce abortion. With purity and holiness I will pass my life and practise my art. I will not cut persons labouring under the stone, but will leave this to be done by men who are practitioners of this work. Into whatever houses I enter, I will go into them for the benefit of the sick, and will abstain from every voluntary act of mischief and corruption; and further, from the seduction of female or males, of freemen and slaves. Whatever, in connection with my professional practice, or not in connection with it, I see or hear, in the life of men, which ought not to be spoken of abroad, I will not divulge, as reckoning that all such should be kept secret. While I continue to keep this Oath unviolated, may it be granted to me to enjoy life and the practice of the art, respected by all men, in all times! But should I trespass and violate this Oath, may the reverse be my lot!"

Introduction

This is a book about facts, statistics, and the future.

Some of the facts come from modern medical and biological science. These are easy to verify, although for those who are laymen in the medical sciences, it will require a little checking of basic textbooks. Many of the facts come directly from the Bible. As such, they are easy to check. Readers who know the Bible and believe what it teaches will find it easy to verify them.

The statistics are a little more problematic. Some of them come from readily available public documents. Others—for example, those prepared by the Center for Disease Control in Atlanta, Georgia, an agency of the Department of Health, Education, and Welfare—have been published recently and are hard to obtain. But the argument does not depend on the *exact* statistics, nor on having them up to the minute. Here too, while some deatils may be in doubt, the general trend is very clear and observers on all sides of the issue admit their validity. There is some dispute about what those statistics mean—and that is where the future comes in. But there is no doubt that they are reliable.

Perhaps you are a student of Scripture or even a highly trained Bible scholar. If so, you will not have to ask yourself whether the basic points made in this book are true. You will only have to decide what they mean to you and what you should do about them. Perhaps you are a doctor, a biology or science teacher, a nurse, or someone else with professional knowledge in the life sciences. If so, you will have no difficulty appreciating the points that will be made about the origin and development of human life prior to birth.

In a way, each of us is part of at least some of the statistics we will be citing. Recently, or perhaps not so recently, every reader has figured in the "live births" column of this or some other nation's vital statistics. Right now each of us stands somewhere in the demographic charts under "age distribution." Sooner or later—unless the record-keeping breaks down—each of us will figure in the "deaths" column.

Some readers or their relatives or close friends, however, may belong in the "abortions" column. For one reason or another they have had an abortion. Or they participated in one as a doctor, nurse, hospital attendant, social worker, or in some other way. Perhaps they are men whose children were aborted, with or without their knowledge or consent. And among the readers there are probably a few whose mothers considered or were advised to have an abortion, but did not. Some of all these knew the full details of what abortion involves; some did not. But anyone who has been involved in an abortion has already been hurt, as I think this book will show. Part of what this book says will add to that hurt. But part of it will show how it can be healed and how you can help prevent others in similar situations from hurting and being hurt.

Finally, there is the future. It is always hard to predict the shape of the future, but some things are rather certain. There is only so much natural gas in the earth's crust. Someday we will run out of it. And the faster we use it, the sooner we will run out. Social Security taxes take a large bite—about six percent—out of every producer's income. As the number of retirees goes up and the number of new producers goes down, that bite is going to have to get bigger. This is not speculation; it is simple mathematical fact. The number of new producers depends on the number of births. And the number of births depends in part on the number of abortions.

Exactly how these trends will turn out, and what they will mean for those already retired, still producing, just coming onto the job market, or the very young is impossible to predict with one hundred percent accuracy. But the general direction in which they are moving our society has to be clear enough, just as the general problem of natural gas and oil is clear enough. How it will turn out in detail—whether it will be bearable, difficult, or

INTRODUCTION

catastrophic—depends on what we do with the possibilities we have. This is true of Social Security, birth, and abortion just as it is of natural gas. So the future—in a real sense, whether there will be a future—depends on our understanding of where we are in the present.

The facts and statistics can be presented with fair accuracy. I have tried to do so in this book. I am confident that they cannot be challenged. There are certain to be errors of detail, as in any human work. But the basic framework simply cannot be challenged. As to the future, what that will be depends on the present and on you, the readers of this book. It depends on whether you understand what America is doing to itself, and on what you have the compassion, the courage, and the wisdom to do about it.

Harold O. J. Brown
Deerfield, Illinois
Ash Wednesday, 1977

1

The Revolution

Perhaps more important than producing 600,000 legal abortions in 1972, the abortion movement affirmed that an act of faith can become revolution.

—Lawrence Lader in *Abortion II* (1973)

What 1972 revolution is abortion activist Lawrence Lader talking about? That was the year before the first major U.S. Supreme Court decision on abortion, *Roe* v. *Wade*.

Roe v. *Wade*

From the mid-1960s through the end of the decade, advocates of permissive abortion were making substantial progress through the state legislatures. In 1971, however, the tide turned. The New York state legislature reversed itself and repealed that state's permissive abortion law; Governor Nelson Rockefeller vetoed the bill and left the permissive law on the books. In 1972, two states, North Dakota and Michigan, held a statewide referendum on liberalized abortion. In both states it was overwhelmingly defeated.

But on January 22, 1973, the United States Supreme Court, in an epoch-making decision, completely turned the tables and gave the pro-abortionists not only all they wanted, but more. *Roe* v. *Wade* in effect permits abortion at any time up to the moment of birth, anywhere in the United States. During the first three months of pregnancy, abortion may not be regulated. During the second trimester, it may be regulated only with reference to the protection of the "mother's" health; in other words, abortion may be subject to certain professional requirements. The Court apparently allowed individual states to restrict abortion during the third trimester, but it left a loophole the size of the proverbial barn door by stipulating that abortion must always be allowed in case of a threat to the mother's health, including her mental health. In other words, even a third-trimester abortion is always available if a physician can be found who will state that the mother's mental health is endangered by her pregnancy. The experience of states such as California with similar "mental health" clauses indicates that, in effect, they permit abortion on demand.

Lader's "revolution" is what happened in New York State as a result of a permissive state abortion law that took effect in 1970. For a brief period, New York City became the abortion capital of the world; journalist Nick Thimmesch reported over half a million abortions in New York City alone during a thirty-month period.[1]

Legal abortions nationwide numbered fewer than 20,000 in 1969. At that time, most states permitted abortion only for grave medical reasons, when continuing a pregnancy meant serious risk to the prospective mother's life. But since the mid-1960s, the pro-abortion movement had succeeded in "liberalizing" abortion restrictions in several states. Before New York passed a law permitting abortion on demand, most liberalization had been in the area of permissible legal reasons for an abortion. The major difference lay in admitting a threat to a prospective mother's "mental health" as grounds for a legal abortion. For several years, many psychiatrists lent themselves more or less voluntarily to approving abortions on the ground of supposed mental or psychological harm a woman might suffer from having a baby.

But in 1970 Lader's "revolution" began. The need for

[1]"The Abortion Culture," *Newsweek*, July 9, 1973, p. 7.

psychiatric approval dropped, at least in New York State. The number of abortions skyrocketed. Psychiatrists lost a little business, but an enterprising group of doctors began to make money. Presbyterian physician and anti-abortion activist William Miller of St. Louis says that short of finding oil on a piece of property, there is no other way land can bring in money as fast as by opening an abortion clinic. From a pro-abortion perspective, psychoanalyst Dr. Magda Denes documents the same fact in her account of New York abortion practices, *In Necessity and Sorrow*.[2]

The U.S. Supreme Court did not legalize abortion on demand nationwide until January 22, 1973, but the revolution had already begun to make itself felt before then. The birth rate, already falling since the "baby boom" of the 1950s, tapered off in the 1960s and began to plummet. And the availability of babies to adopt slackened almost overnight. Christian, private, and public homes, agencies, and services that had ministered to pregnant women, their babies, and tens of thousands of hopeful adoptive parents suddenly found themselves "unwanted." All across the country, such agencies closed their doors in the early 1970s. A few struggled on. Some transformed themselves into "pregnancy counseling services"—usually a euphemism for abortion referral. A small number went the whole way and became abortion clinics.

Social Response

As this trend was sweeping the nation, a few exceptions stood out. Some agencies kept their doors open and continued to help unmarried, pregnant girls bring their children into the world and place them for adoption.

Many of the propagandists of "sexual liberation" (who are also usually advocates of liberal abortion) charge that the "puritanical" and "hypocritical" sexual attitudes of "outmoded" popula-

[2]Magda Denes, *In Necessity and Sorrow: Life and Death in an Abortion Hospital* (New York: Basic Books, 1976).

16

tion groups—evangelical Protestants, conservative Roman Catholics, and Mormons, to name but three—*cause* much of the problem of unwanted pregnancies by fighting birth control and sex education. But strangely enough, the girls from such "puritanical" groups were the ones who had the courage and compassion to keep their pregnancies in the years when those who were "with it," who considered sex outside marriage natural and no disgrace, were flocking to abortion clinics.

There can be no doubt that much suffering has been caused by intolerant, judgmental attitudes of many Christians. And many Christian girls, finding themselves pregnant out of wedlock, have felt compelled to disappear quietly, go to an abortion clinic, and have their pregnancies "terminated" because they thought they would encounter nothing but condemnation and hostility among their fellow Christians. Unfortunately, Christian parents have sometimes given a daughter the impression it would be far better for her to slip away for an abortion than ever to admit having had sexual relations before marriage. Sometimes it hasn't been verbalized, but it has been communicated. And the effect is the same.

Nevertheless, it is true that while many non-Christian adoption agencies were forced to close, a few Christian agencies were able to keep going. At least some of the girls who could not resist the pressure-cooker temptations of modern life and so became pregnant outside of marriage *were* able to resist society's offer of a "safe, legal" way out. Increasingly, individual Christians and whole congregations are coming to see that unwanted pregnancies provide an occasion for a ministry of compassion and love. A compassionate witness and ministry to a girl with a pregnancy she thinks she cannot keep can be a blessing to her, to a baby, and usually to hopeful adoptive parents. Hostility and condemnation are a blessing to no one—except, in financial terms at least, to those who "strike gold" in abortion clinics.

When young Christians yield to sexual temptation and an unwanted pregnancy results, it only reveals that not one of us lives up to God's standards—"For all have sinned, and come short of the glory of God" (Rom. 3:23). For older (it would be wrong to say "more mature") Christians to put such young people under pressure to "cover it up" and "get rid of it" by any means possible is worse. C. S. Lewis has argued that sexual sins are usually abuses of love, but spiritual sins such as pride show an absence of love.

As Professor I. C. Bernstein of the University of Minnesota Medical School told a congressional subcommittee in March, 1976, society must be able to do more for an unmarried, pregnant girl than just help her "get rid" of the baby by an abortion. There *is* something better, but it takes more money, more time, more personal attention, and—unlike the abortion business—operates at a deficit instead of a profit. It is no credit to God's people that many Christians engage in extramarital sex and have out-of-wedlock pregnancies. But it *is* a credit to Christians that there are families, ministers, churches, and groups who know how to minister to pregnant girls and to the boys involved with them. They do this with Jesus' combination of law and love, rather than with the world's anonymity and indifference.

But a compassionate few, by their good example, can hardly buck a nationwide wave endorsed by the Supreme Court, advocated by most of the media, and paid for by tax dollars. And the result is an increase from 20,000 legal abortions in 1969 to almost 900,000 in 1974—the last year for which authoritative statistics are available. Estimates for 1975 and 1976 exceed 1 million. In smaller communities such as Washington, D.C., more up-to-date statistics are available and the figures are startling. In 1976, the year of both the Bicentennial and the evangelical, there were more abortions in Washington than live births. And of live births, more were born out of wedlock than to married couples.

Births in the United States in 1975 barely exceeded 3.1 million (down from a high of 4.3 million in the late 1950s). In 1975, according to Planned Parenthood—World Population, 400,000–900,000 American women who "needed" abortions could not get them because of local pressure, medical obstinacy, or bureaucratic obstruction. If we take the high figure— 900,000—and assume the abortions had been obtained, births in America would have dropped to 2.2 million in 1975 and the number of abortions would almost have matched that of births.

A Last Resort?

When the pro-abortion movement began to gather momentum in the 1960s, most abortion advocates presented it as a regrettable but necessary "last resort." In general, it was denied that the developing fetus is human life "in the full sense." The U.S. Supreme Court, in its revolutionary abortion decision, *Roe v. Wade*, adopts this unscientific, essentially obscurantist position. Such a position at least has the merit of preserving the appearance of ethical decency, however, for if the developing child is less than human, then killing it must always be less than homicide (from the Latin *homo*, "human being," and *occidere*, "kill"; homicide means manslaying, killing a human). However, more and more pro-abortionists are admitting quite openly that an abortion destroys a human life. The fiction adopted by the Supreme Court is openly repudiated by most of those who now hail its abortion decision.

> 'The right-to-lifers' argument is simple: a fetus is a human life, and the government should not sanction the taking of human life except in the direst circumstances, such as when another life is threatened. None of the common pro-abortion arguments deal with this issue head-on. Would "a woman's right to control her own body" permit her to kill another adult person who has committed no offense against her? Would we sanction the murder of children who are unwanted and unloved, just as we sanction the destruction of fetuses because they *might turn out* that way? Would it evoke much sympathy for a "legalize terror bombing" movement, to be told that terrorists often injure themselves with amateurish home-made bombs? (italics added).

Despite this very clear acknowledgement of what goes on in abortion, this *New Republic* editorial favors abortion. It continues:

DEATH BEFORE BIRTH

Those who believe a woman should be free to have an abortion must face the consequences of their beliefs. Metaphysical arguments about the beginning of life are fruitless. But there clearly is no logical or moral distinction between a fetus and a young baby; free availability of abortion cannot be reasonably distinguished from euthanasia.

No anti-abortionist could put the matter more clearly. How astonishing, then, is the editorial's conclusion:

Nevertheless, we are for it. It is too facile to say that human life is always sacred; obviously it is not, and the social cost of preserving against the mother's will the lives of fetuses who are not yet self-conscious is simply too great.[3]

Dr. Magda Denes, author of *In Necessity and Sorrow: Life and Death in an Abortion Hospital*, documents in page after page of interviews and description what the *New Republic* essentially affirmed. Indeed, the very use of the term "death" in a book dealing with abortion is clear evidence that Dr. Denes, like the physicians and health care workers she interviews, knows quite well what is going on. But despite the fact that she documents several cases where the abortion is clearly sought for trivial reasons of personal convenience, she calls every abortion, for whatever reason, a case of "absolute necessity."[4]

In many ways the testimony of this New York psychologist of Hungarian Jewish background, with her memories of the a-trocities of World War II, is itself a testimony to the tragic predicament caused by the abortion controversy, abortion, and its aftermath. Magda Denes herself had an abortion, as she describes in the opening pages of her book. Indeed, the reader will immediately suspect that the book is a form of personal confession. Dr. Denes writes as though she must exorcise the lie that abortion is not killing, leaving herself and all those who are

[3]*The New Republic*, July 2, 1977, pp. 5-6.
[4]Denes, *In Necessity and Sorrow*, p. 247.

involved in it only the excuse of "necessity" in a world characterized by absurdity.

Because she does support abortion, Dr. Denes was unwilling to allow her material to be used in this book, a relatively unusual reluctance where scholarly material such as hers is concerned. Because of her honesty, she could not help testifying to what she knew. Nevertheless, because of the ambiguities of her own situation and perhaps out of consideration for the millions who have abortions but lack her own ability to look the facts in the face, she refused permission to draw upon her book for documentation of our position here. Thus a second time she bears witness to the terrible moral abyss into which abortion can plunge one: her book is a testimony which in a sense she does not want to be received; the attention it receives will create a response she does not want to see spread. Yet she wrote it, and continues to write and speak "in favor" of abortion, all the while clearly labeling it "killing."

Magda Denes deserves our recognition for her remarkable and terribly significant testimony. If many of her readers hope she will eventually reach a different conclusion from that of her book, they are really only hoping she may ultimately work out the implications of the intense moral and spiritual uneasiness to which *In Necessity and Sorrow* is such eloquent witness.

We may not accept her contention that all abortions are cases of absolute necessity. But are any? What about the cases in which, since the beginning of the Christian era, abortion has been reluctantly permitted — the cases in which the mother's life is at stake?

Danger of Maternal Death

Ever since the beginnings of the specialty of gynecology under Soranus of Ephesus, a second-century physician, attention has been given to situations in which a pregnancy threatens a mother's life. The classic case is one in which the head of the fetus is too large to pass through the mother's birth canal. In such a situation, labor cannot be completed and both mother and baby will die. Soranus describes the situation and prescribes abortion as the only way to save at least one life. (The "Caesarean" section, named for Julius Caesar who was delivered by it, was used when the mother died in childbirth. With ancient operating techniques, it was not possible to have a modern Caesarean section, for abdominal operations could not be performed without fatal consequences.)

Two things must be noted about the abortion performed to save the mother's life. First, when such a desperate situation really occurs, Jewish and Christian ethics agree with Soranus. They have consistently taught that such an abortion *is* permissible. Tertullian, a third-century Christian theologian, wrote that in such a case, the baby's life must be taken "by a necessary cruelty . . . lest it become its mother's murderer."[5] Tertullian's verdict is consistent with that of the early church and with Orthodox rabbinical teaching—taking an innocent life is always an evil, but in this desperate situation it is permissible. *Some* Roman Catholic writers in the last two centuries have claimed that abortion is forbidden by God's laws even under these circumstances, but their interpretation is not consistent with historic Christian teaching.

Second, given modern medical techniques, almost never does a pregnancy threaten to take the mother's life today. Alan F. Guttmacher, M.D., author of noted textbooks on gynecology, late head of Planned Parenthood–World Population, and a vigorous pro-abortionist, wrote in his standard text that there are no situations today in which the mother's life cannot be saved without taking the baby's—except in cases where the mother will probably die whatever the doctors do.[6]

The modern Caesarean delivery saves *both* the baby and the mother, except when the baby is "unwanted." Then the same

[5]Tertullian, *De anima*, xxxvii.
[6]Alan F. Guttmacher, M.D., and Joseph J. Rovinsky, M.D., eds., *Medical, Surgical, and Gynecological Complications of Pregnancy*, 1st and 2nd ed. (Baltimore: Williams & Wilkins, 1960 and 1965), esp. pp. 29, 127, 310, 560; cf. 2nd ed., pp. 35-36.

operation is called a hysterotomy (a form of abortion) and produces a dead baby because the baby is allowed to die or has its blood and oxygen supply cut off shortly before delivery. Almost all other cases are treatable by various medical and surgical means short of taking the baby's life unless, as already noted, the problem is so severe it will kill the mother in any case.

One exception to Dr. Guttmacher's statement is what is called an *ectopic* pregnancy (from Greek *ek,* "out of," and *topos,* "place"). In an ectopic pregnancy the embryo begins to develop in the Fallopian tube rather than in the flexible uterus. An ectopic pregnancy simply cannot produce a live child in the present state of modern medicine. (Perhaps some day it will be possible to save such an embryo, but it is not possible yet.) An ectopic pregnancy inevitably will cause the Fallopian tube to burst; almost invariably that kills the mother.

But Guttmacher does not include this condition under the types of pregnancy that might require an abortion because such an operation is considered major abdominal surgery, not abortion. (The *purpose* of an abortion, as we shall see, is to insure that *no child is born.* The purpose of surgery to remove an ectopic pregnancy is strictly to save the mother's life.)

Thus the cases in which an abortion genuinely seems to be required to save the mother's life have fallen virtually to zero, thanks to modern medicine. Where such a case does arise, law, religion, and medical ethics all permit an abortion. The rarity of such cases is shown by the fact that prior to 1969, when this type of abortion was legal throughout the United States while abortion for other reasons generally was not, abortions nationwide numbered fewer than 20,000.

Therapeutic Abortions

In older medical books, "abortions" were divided into two classes—"spontaneous" and "therapeutic." A "spontaneous" abortion is called a miscarriage in everyday language. A "therapeutic" abortion (from Greek *therapeia,* "treatment, cure") was deliberately undertaken for medical reasons, generally to save the mother's life.

But because the vast majority of present-day abortions cannot be called "therapeutic," since they do not represent treatment or cure for a *disease,* the term "spontaneous abortion" for miscarriage has been largely abandoned and medical abortions are now classified as "therapeutic" (where there is a serious threat to the mother's health) and "elective" (meaning one that was desired although not medically required). Since modern medical skills make genuine therapeutic abortions very rare if not altogether nonexistent, almost all abortions in American today are "elective"—freely chosen.

Indications

Today, of course—to use Associate Justice White's phrase in his dissent in *Roe* v. *Wade*—abortion is legal in America "for any . . . reason or for no reason." But before general legalization, abortion advocates were arguing that abortion ought to be permitted on the basis of certain "indications." These indications range all the way from the medical problem of the mother's life—where virtually all authorities have agreed an abortion may be performed—to what are called "social" indications, which may mean nothing more than that the prospective mother or parents will find the child inconvenient. Let's look at them individually.

There are four general categories of "indications" that have been put forward as justification for abortion. The first category, "medical," we have already briefly considered. The second category, "eugenic," involves cases in which it is known or thought that a defective child will be born. (Sometimes these cases are also called "medical," but it makes more sense to call them "eugenic" because the intention is not to treat the mother medically but to eliminate a defective child and thus "improve the race"—from Greek *eu,* "good," and *genos,* "race.")

The third category is "criminal" and involves pregnancy as a result of rape or incest. Pregnancies resulting from forcible rape are very rare, but they do occur. They present a special kind of problem, as do pregnancies resulting from incest. The final category, "social," begins with psychological and mental stress, includes financial and family hardship—as in cases where a poor family already has several children—and finally embraces all those cases in which the expected child is unwanted. Cases of genuine psychological disturbance, however, may be considered as "medical" indications.

Medical Indications

What about the remaining medical indications, apart from an actual threat to the life of the mother? In general, they can be dealt with without need for an abortion. Advances in medical science that help women who have difficulty bringing children into the world often also benefit women whose health is impaired by a pregnancy. During the early phase of abortion liberalization, "psychiatric" indications were added to the medical ones.

There can be no doubt that for many women a pregnancy causes severe psychological stress. Indeed, this often happens with wanted pregnancies. The most commonly-cited problem—a pregnant woman who appears despondent and perhaps even threatens to commit suicide—is far more often a pretext than a genuine psychiatric indication. Statistics show that pregnant women are among the most *unlikely* candidates for suicide.[7]

It is fair to say there is no sound psychiatric evidence that abortion helps a mentally disturbed patient, and certainly not enough to justify the taking of a life. In fact, the opposite may well be true: an abortion may increase a patient's mental distress. Moreover, it is fairly generally admitted among psychiatrists and other medical personnel that the "psychiatric indica-

[7]Cf. Samuel A. Nigro, M.D., "Abortion," Journal of the American Medical Association (JAMA), Vol. 219:8 (February 21, 1972), p. 1068.

tions" were usually just a subterfuge to permit an abortion for which there was no genuine medical indication.[8] Since abortions have become legal nationwide, psychiatric indications have virtually disappeared. However, as we shall see, the problem of psychiatric complications due to abortion has by no means disappeared.

"Eugenic" Indications

Since the word "eugenics" is suggestive of Nazi doctrines of racial superiority, it is often avoided. The expression "prevention of fetal deformities" or "prevention of birth defects" is substituted. Like so many expressions in the modern world, "prevention of defects" is a kind of Newspeak that conceals what it really means. Certainly no one could be in favor of "promotion of birth defects." How can anyone be against their "prevention"? The answer, of course, lies in what this euphemism actually means, namely, "prevention of defectives." In fact, the "defectives" are not "prevented," but rather *eliminated*.

The "eugenic" problem has to be seen from two sides: (1) the implications for the individual, and (2) the implications for society. No one who has suffered a severe handicap or who has had a severely handicapped person in his family or among his close friends can fail to understand and appreciate the suffering, the heartbreak, and the financial and physical burdens one or more severe handicaps can cause. (Birth defects frequently appear in multiples, rather than singly.) A person who has lived with a handicap himself or with a handicapped person may also understand that such a handicap can provide an occasion for courage, selflessness, creative love, and ultimately for building character.

---

[8]On January 21, 1973, the eve of the announcement of the *Roe* v. *Wade* decision, I participated in a symposium in New York sponsored by the Christian Medical Society. One of the psychiatrists said, in effect, "Let's admit it. Over ninety percent of the psychiatric authorizations are based on nothing more than the patient's desire to have an abortion." No one contradicted him.

THE REVOLUTION

But it is one thing to take such a burden on oneself, and quite another to make someone else take it on *himself*, or—since the mother usually bears the greater burden of dealing with a handicapped child—on *herself*. And there are handicaps that are so severe it is hard to see how anyone can benefit from them in any way.

(1) Implications for the Individual

There are two kinds of individuals involved in fetal deformity or birth defects: first, the individual who has the defect, and second, those individuals—parents, family members, perhaps health care professionals and social workers—who care for him.

It is frequently suggested that a defective individual would be "better off dead" or never born because his life "isn't worth living." As German psychiatrist Helmut E. Ehrhardt points out, to make that decision for another person usurps his moral responsibility. It is evident that most handicapped and defective individuals do value their lives, however undesirable they may seem to those who are "normal." In fact, the number of suicides among the handicapped is lower than among the general population.

It is really the second group—parents and family—with whom most of those worried about "prevention of defects" are concerned. And although a handicapped or deformed child frequently brings unexpected blessings and joy,[9] it is impossible to minimize the burden that lifelong care may cause. However, if society is really concerned about the parents, brothers, sisters, and other relatives of a handicapped person, there is a great deal that can be done—especially in our rich society—short of taking that person's life. But most of it is very expensive.

[9]See the testimony in *The Right to Live: The Right to Die* (Wheaton: Tyndale, 1976) of Christian surgeon C. Everett Koop, who has treated more "defective" children in thirty years of specialization than any other living physician. Regarding the desire of deformed children to live as well as the surprising happiness they may bring to others, see Eugene F. Diamond, M.D., "The Deformed Child's Right to Life," in Dennis J. Horan and David Mall, eds., *Death, Dying, and Euthanasia* (Washington: University Publications, 1977).

DEATH BEFORE BIRTH

(2) Implications for Society

When politicians, administrators, or political theorists begin to talk about the "high cost" of caring for certain "defectives," watch out. When the defectives are said to have no "meaningful life," you can be sure what the next step is: "prevent" them—that is, kill them or let them die. When eugenics is taken to mean trying to help people produce healthy children, it is unobjectionable. But if it is taken to mean "improving the race" by eliminating those who are "substandard," it does not take much imagination to see that it must lead to euthansia.

Criminal Indications

One of the more difficult arguments to handle is that of forcible rape or incest. These are sometimes referred to as "criminal" indications, inasmuch as the pregnancy results from a criminal act. From the point of view of law, the pregnancy should never have happened and its continuation represents an ongoing offense against the girl who has been raped or forced to submit to incestuous intercourse. As a practical matter, it may be pointed out that the number of actual cases of pregnancy arising from forcible rape is very small. In theory, too, one might say that if forcible rape or incest has been established, there ought to be criminal action against the responsible party, quite independent of the abortion question. There is no doubt that these two offenses pose tremendous problems for the victim, her family, and—if it is allowed to be born—the child.

Although the case of rape seems to be one in which abortion might logically be allowed, since otherwise pregnancy and birth are forced on the woman by violence, there are a number of reasons why it is not wise to make rape legal grounds for abortion.

First, there is the matter of binding legal evidence. Rape is a crime, one that is often difficult to prove. If legal proof is demanded as a condition for the abortion, then providing the proof will generally take so long that it will be too late for an abortion. If binding legal proof is not demanded, then the mere claim of rape, not proof of rape, becomes the prerequisite for an abortion. Thus, from the perspective of a meaningful legal requirement, the exception for rape leaves much to be desired.

Second, if a rape has occurred and is promptly reported, immediate medical attention prevents pregnancy, as indicated by studies of 4,800 rape victims in the St. Paul-Minneapolis area.[10]

Third, even though the abortion is intended to protect the woman who is pregnant against her will, it destroys a developing child, thus causing an innocent party to suffer for the misdeed of another.

Fourth, *if* the intent really is to help the injured woman (and not merely to save society money) then there are better things that can be done for her than destroying the child, which may bring on further emotional and psychological shock. Those better things—personal care, love, perhaps psychiatric help— are all more expensive and time-consuming than the abortion.

Fifth, because society appears to save money on an abortion since it is cheaper than counseling, placement, and psychiatric help, its motives in urging abortion for the rape victim may be economic self-interest, not compassion.

It would be wrong to overlook the genuine and terrible problems that rape presents, particularly in those cases—fortunately very few in number—where a pregnancy results. If a woman in distress asks for an abortion because the child was conceived through a rape, relatives and friends should seek to sympathize with her and support her, even as they try to provide her with a better and more compassionate "solution" than abortion. When the state, on the other hand, urges abortion as being so much more "economical" than birth, it would be naive not to suspect

[10]John F. Hillabrand, "Dealing With a Rape Case," *Heartbeat*, Vol. 8 (March, 1975), p. 250.

its motives.[11] When reasons of "economy" become the decisive factor in questions of life and death, look out! Who among us can be sure he has produced more for society than he has cost? Or that he always will? Admittedly, this does not refute the argument that a criminal indication might be a valid reason for an abortion, but it should make us very cautious of accepting abortion in cases of rape and incest. If we accept the principle that a person's cost to society determines his right to live, we may be curing more than we think.

These arguments are not intended to be used with a shattered victim of forcible rape. But the rape victims do not make the laws. Most of the time our lawmakers, such as the seven Supreme Court justices who voted for abortion in *Roe* v. *Wade,* are supposed to have time for mature reflection and consideration. They are the ones who should be persuaded to listen to these considerations and to take them seriously. "Hard cases make bad law," the proverb says. Before we hastily accept abortion as a solution to the admittedly hard case of rape-caused pregnancy, let us take the time to analyze what such a solution implies about our values and what it may portend for the future of a nation that measures the value of life, even of unborn life, in terms of cost effectiveness.

Social Indications

The term "social indications" refers to a variety of circumstances that may affect a couple's or a woman's ability or willingness to care for a child. Examples of social indications are poverty, the presence of an "excessive" number of children in the family, "too great" a gap between the last child born and the one now expected, and parents who are "too old" to want to

---

[11]In Senate debate on federal funding of "elective" (medically unnecessary) abortions, Senator Charles H. Percy (R., Ill.) spoke enthusiastically of the "cost effectiveness" of abortions as opposed to welfare aid to dependent children. Cf. *Congressional Record,* June 29, 1977. Paradoxically, Senator Percy himself was a "dependent child," supported in part by welfare.

assume the burden of a new baby. All of these "social indications" are relative, and the seriousness with which they are viewed will vary from person to person and from situation to situation. It is generally admitted that the so-called "social indications" really represent the transition from supposedly medical indications to what is in effect abortion on demand. Thus the Scandinavians, instead of speaking of "social indications," refer to "self-determined" abortion. By this they tacitly recognize that calling such relative, hard-to-weigh factors "indications" is really to say that a woman may have an abortion if she really wants it.

From 20,000 to 1,000,000 plus . . .

The rise in the number of abortions from 1969 to 1975, from 20,000 to 1 million or so, is a five thousand percent increase. If we were to simply make a straight-line projection, we could say that in about ten years every female in the United States, from newborn babies to the very oldest ladies, would have received two abortions each. Of course, this is silly. But it is evident that abortion on demand is becoming a "way of life" to increasing numbers of Americans. It makes a very good life, at least in financial terms, for the small number of physicians who specialize in it. And it is a "way of death" for increasing numbers of the youngest human beings in America each year.

In 1975, more deaths were caused by abortions than any other cause: heart disease took only eight percent as many lives as abortions did. Approximately one in four babies conceived in 1975 was killed "safely and legally" before birth by a physician, at the "mother's" request. There is no doubt that a revolution is under way, and we are in the middle of it. What kind of society is this revolution producing?

2

Life After the Revolution

Whom the gods would destroy, they first make mad.

—Euripedes

The revolution is coming. In fact, as Lawrence Lader claimed in 1973, it is already here. But what will life be like after the revolution? Will America after the abortion revolution discover (as Russia did after the Communist revolution) that the reality looks a lot different from the revolutionary slogans? Clearly we have to get beyond slogans to the reality if we are to deal intelligently with our problems and have a chance for a hopeful future.

Newspeak: Theirs and Ours

As an English wit remarked, "Orthodoxy is *our* doxy—heterodoxy is *your* doxy." We have already pointed out how the language of the pro-abortionists contains euphemisms to conceal realities: "prevention of birth defects" instead of "elimination of defectives," to name but one. These euphemisms run all through the pro-abortion movement. The woman who seeks an abortion is regularly referred to as "the mother," although logically she can't be a mother without the existence of a child, whose presence is regularly denied. The words "child" and "baby" are shunned. Instead, "fetus" and "embryo" are used. Today we are getting used to even more distant circumlocutions: "abortus" and "product of conception." Actually, the word "fetus" is Latin for "suckling" or "young one." And so for people who know Latin, it is no more comfortable to kill a "fetus" than a "baby."

On the other hand, in many situations the strong words crop back up again. Most anti-abortionists do not call abortion "murder." "Murder" is usually used for the deliberate, premeditated killing of an innocent human being. A legal execution is not murder; accidental homicide is not murder; and, from the point of view of legal language, abortion has always had so many complicating factors that most anti-abortionists hesitate to call it murder, although they all will call it killing. The term "murder" does crop up, however, in the abortion hospitals where, as Dr. Denes reports, the personnel frequently use it bitterly or sardonically to describe their work.[1]

And the term "baby" surfaces in remarkable ways. When a pregnant woman expresses doubt about going through an abortion and a social worker suggests giving the child up for adoption, frequently the "mother" replies, "Oh, I couldn't give up my *baby*." That is the only time, commented a worker, that they call it a baby. Otherwise, when arranging to have it "terminated," they scrupulously avoid the term.[2]

While anti-abortionists do not like the expressions "fetus" and "abortus" (Latin for "aborted one") because of their connotations, although the terms are admittedly technically correct, pro-abortionists detest the terms "murder," "person," "baby," and "human being." They detest them because of their implications and sometimes will claim they are incorrect. However, a surprising number of pro-abortionists, like Dr. Denes and the abortionists she describes, are increasingly frank in using them.

Are they correct? We have already mentioned that "murder" generally refers to premeditated killing and is not generally used by anti-abortionists. Like "murder," "person" is a legal term, not a natural or philosophical one. A person is what the

[1]Denes, *In Necessity and Sorrow,* p. 57.
[2]Cf. Ibid., pp. 76-77.

law declares to be a person. Corporations are persons. For the first eighty years of our national existence, Negro slaves were non-persons. Unborn children have generally not been explicitly called "persons," although they did possess some legal rights. Now the Supreme Court, in *Roe* v. *Wade,* has defined them as "non-persons."

Since "person" is a technical legal term, it is not very practical. It is quite enough to make the point with the more natural expressions "baby" and "human being." "Baby" is simply a descriptive term applied to the littlest or youngest members of any class. Thus we have baby ducks and baby elephants. When the candidate for abortion is called a "baby," it is clear enough that it is a baby *something.* But a baby what? At this point we come to the philosophical expression "human being." On this term the anti-abortion case stands or falls.

What is a "being"? A being is a living *entity;* in fact, entity is an English word derived from the Latin *ens,* the participle meaning "being." An entity has individuality, distinctiveness, and a measure of permanence or continuity. The fetus is clearly a being, because it is there and it is alive. Unlike the male sperm and the female ovum that combine to make it, the fetus has an individual, distinct existence and a future; it will continue to live for a relatively long time if not destroyed by sickness or injury. The spermatozoön has no continuity apart from an ovum with which it can unite, and the ovum has no continuity apart from a sperm. They are *living,* it is true, but they are not "beings." The fetus, in contrast, is a "being." Left to itself, it will develop and demonstrate that it is an individual with a personal destiny. And what kind of a being is it? At the risk of sounding somewhat elementary, we will say it is neither vegetable nor mineral; it is of the *animal* family. And what kind of an animal? Clearly it is not a fish, nor a fowl, nor anything else but *human.* Linguistically, medically, and philosophically it makes perfect sense to call the fetus a human being, and it is silly to pretend its genuine humanness can be ignored by calling it a "fetus," "abortus," or "product of conception."

LIFE AFTER THE REVOLUTION

The French now permit abortion, although on a much more limited basis than the United States. But they know perfectly well what is being aborted. Their new law calls it *un être humain*—a human being. The same thing is true of Germans, who have no difficulty calling the fetus *ein menschliches Wesen*—a human being. This may sound like quibbling over words, but it really isn't. Part of Hitler's technique in persuading the German people to close their eyes to his extermination policies was to call the lives of those he killed *wertlos* ("worthless") and *menschenunwürdig* ("without human value or dignity").

But whether the argument involves us in Newspeak or not, it is apparent that at the moment the pro-abortionists are having it all their own way. More than 1 million abortions per year, paid for in large measure at public expense (about one-third by Medicaid and many more by private health insurance), prove that. Whatever we call it—"human being," "*être humain*," "product of conception," or "*wertlos*"—hundreds of thousands are being destroyed each year in America.

A Revolution?

If by "revolution" we mean "big change," then maybe the abortion situation isn't a revolution yet. In 1969, apart from accidental miscarriages, 99.5 percent of babies conceived were delivered. In 1975, apart from miscarriages, the figure was still over 75 percent. Most of the conceived babies are still "wanted" and "born."

What would you think of a religion that made 1 million converts in America each year? Even if a certain percentage of those "converted" were repeaters, it is evident that at a million-a-year rate the whole country would soon be under the control of whatever philosophy the religion represented.

In one sense, having an abortion may seem different from making a religious decision. The person seeking an abortion is in trouble and is looking for a way out. She is not looking for a new philosophy or religion. But in many senses, having an abortion *is* a similar action.

DEATH BEFORE BIRTH

There is an apocryphal story in India that the first thing the Christians get a Hindu to do when he is converted to Christianity is to eat a piece of meat and drink a glass of whiskey. The Hindus are implying that no one could possibly want to become a Christian except to "enjoy" those vices that Hindus detest: "cow murder," as they call it, and alcohol.[3]

What happens in an abortion is a bit like what Hindus think happens when a converted Hindu eats a piece of beef: he has broken with the fundamental concept of the sacredness of the cow. Even though he may not understand the implications of what he has done, he has moved from one way of thinking to another, and the beef-eating pretty well makes it definite. The woman who submits to an abortion may not be aware of moving from one philosophy of human life to another. Probably the religious and philosophical implications of it all are not very clear to her. But by her action she has moved from the large camp of those who think all human life has value and is worth protecting to the smaller but growing camp of those who think its value is dependent on other things—its "meaningfulness" or "wantedness."

The doctors, social workers, jurists, and others who are actively involved in making abortion possible ought to better understand the implications of what they are doing. Some of them do. There have been a few celebrated "conversions" from the abortion on demand mentality. Among them is Bernard Nathanson, M.D., of New York City. Dr. Nathanson, a founder of one of New York's first, biggest, and most lucrative abortion "facilities," the so-called "Center for Reproductive Health," dropped out of the abortion business when he became con-

---

[3]Like most popular tales, this one has a grain of truth. Some missionaries have encouraged converts from Hinduism to eat meat in order to show they have repudiated the Hindu belief in reincarnation. This is not common, however. In fact, many Christians in India practice vegetarianism so they will not alienate Hindus. And I have never encountered a missionary who offered converts a drink of whiskey!

vinced he had participated in sixty-thousand deaths.[4] But even Dr. Nathanson has not publicly demonstrated that he *fully* understands. He has dropped out and he admits abortion to be the taking of human life, but he feels the business should go on—only without him.

Jurists who have once taken the pro-abortion position seem to find it difficult to change. Associate Justice Harry A. Blackmun, who wrote the *Roe* v. *Wade* decision as well as other pro-abortion decisions, made a number of statements in *Roe* v. *Wade* that simply are inaccurate. This has been pointed out by jurists, medical personnel, and scholars from all over the world and from all sides of the religious and philosophical spectrum—even by pro-abortionists. But Blackmun, although occasionally showing he has misgivings, has never publicly acknowledged or commented on any of the factual criticism of his action. He has commented on what he calls "hate mail," but has never reflected on what he might have done to incur such hatred.

Although some women are repeaters (accurate figures on the number of second and later abortions are impossible to obtain), few are eager to have even one abortion. In Magda Denes's survey of one New York hospital, the vast majority of abortion patients were there for a first abortion. It is safe to assume the majority of our country's million-plus annual abortion patients are first-timers. Even if we assume that only two-thirds are first abortions, this would provide us with more than 3 million new abortion patients since legalization (sixty percent of an estimated 5 million).[5] If this continues, we can look forward to the time not so many years from now when one-quarter, one-third, or even one-half of American women will have voluntarily destroyed a developing *être humain* by abortion. And of course an equal

[4]Bernard N. Nathanson, "Deeper into Abortion," *New England Journal of Medicine,* Vol. 291:22 (Nov. 28, 1974), pp. 1189–90.

[5]Official H.E.W. figures, available only through 1974 at this writing, indicate about 2 million abortions since New York's abortion mills went into action in 1970. The rate in 1975, 1976, and 1977 is expected to average at least 1 million per year.

number of men will be involved, through causing the pregnancy and advising or consenting to the abortion. In addition, many medical and health care personnel, social workers, and others are directly involved.

Conversion from What to What?

Conversion signifies a turning *away* from something *toward* something else. Christian conversion means turning away from sin to God and the fruit of the Spirit. What is "abortion conversion"?

It is clear enough what the pro-abortionists are turning *from.* They are turning away from the Judaeo-Christian view that man was made in the image of God. According to the standard textbook *A History of Western Morals,* from the moment Christianity came on the scene in the ancient world, abortion rapidly declined and disappeared.[6] Early Christians, who understood that human beings are not absurd accidents of space, time, and chance, but rather are creations in God's image, considered abortion an atrocity. Christian writers condemned it, but they did not have to write extensively about it. It died out just as did infanticide, which in those times was the practice of abandoning unwanted babies to be eaten by wild beasts or to die of exposure.

The pro-abortionists are not only turning away from Judaeo-Christian ethics. They are also turning away from the highest standard of medical ethics, as exemplified by the Oath of Hippocrates. This Oath was actually written under the influence of a pagan philosophical school, that of Pythagoras. As the Supreme Court itself acknowledged, the Oath was universally accepted in the early Roman Empire thanks to the rising influence of Christianity. Ludwig Edelstein, the great classical historian, pointed out that the Pythagoreans, like the Jews and Christians, believed man is made in the image of God. Hence their

[6]William E. H. Lecky, *A History of Western Morals* (New York: Braziller, 1955), pp. 20–24.

Hippocratic Oath expressly rules out abortion and suicide and it was readily endorsed by Christians.[7]

Anyone who practices abortion must necessarily repudiate the Hippocratic Oath. The U.S. Supreme Court was very clear about this, as we will see in our discussion of *Roe* v. *Wade*. For medicine to drop the Hippocratic Oath is to abandon a fundamental statement of the philosophic basis for the practice of medicine. Almost without exception doctors have, until recently, accepted the Hippocratic Oath.[8] However, following the Supreme Court decision of 1973, the Oath quickly began to be phased out. One medical school has introduced a new promise in place of the old one to "give no deadly drug, nor . . . a pessary to produce an abortion." Its graduates now promise to "do nothing illegal." (Apparently no one has noticed that the atrocities performed by German physicians in the concentration camps were all perfectly *legal,* according to the laws in force at the time.)

The "abortion revolution" then involves throwing out the Hippocratic Oath and the biblical conviction that man is made in God's image. And out with the Oath go also the prohibitions against "deadly drugs" and "suicide." The first duty of physicians, under the old Hippocratic ethic, was never knowingly to do harm. Today, only four full years after abortion on demand, more and more doctors are willing to kill their patients. What used to seem an atrocity is gradually becoming familiar, bearable, and even desirable.

If physicians, social services, and ordinary humans are being converted in great numbers, either by undergoing an abortion, taking part in one, or making money from one, what are they being converted *to?* This is more difficult to say. Professor Gregory Casey of the University of Missouri's School of Journalism, in a study of the attitudes of pro- and anti-abortionists,

[7]Cf. Ludwig Edelstein, *The Hippocratic Oath, Supplements to the Bulletin of the History of Medicine*, No. 1, ed. Henry E. Sigerist (Baltimore: Johns Hopkins, 1943).

[8]For the traditional text of the Oath of Hippocrates, see frontispiece.

found that the anti-abortionists almost all shared a common spiritual or philosophical starting point. They all believed that man is made in the image of God and that for this reason the wanton destruction of developing human life is a terrible crime.

The anti-abortionists, however, found it difficult to agree on tactics; most demanded a so-called Human Life Amendment guaranteeing legal protection to all developing babies. Others were willing to accept a States' Rights Amendment, which would simply return to the state legislatures the power to control abortion. And a small number felt, for various reasons, that it was useless to try to influence the state and that they can only protest without changing anything.

Turning to the pro-abortionists, he found a bewildering variety of reasons for supporting abortion—everything from believing abortion is an atrocity that cannot be prevented and hence should be allowed under "hygienic" conditions, to those like Lader and a few others who appear to see in each abortion a "triumph of the human spirit." But since the Supreme Court has given the pro-abortionists more than they could possibly want, all they have to do to keep their victory is to prevent any changes. There is no religious or philosophical unity among them, but there doesn't have to be. They can unite in blocking change. And this they have done so far quite successfully.

I Believe in Abortion?

Thus the question, "To what are the pro-abortionists converted?" is impossible to answer. Almost no one will say he or she believes abortion is a good thing. The usual argument is that it is an unfortunate necessity. However, it is not reasonable to suggest that a large segment of civilization is simply throwing out three thousand years of biblical ethics to replace it with nothing. There must be, consciously or unconsciously, some other value that appears more important to pro-abortionists than the old view of the value of human life made in God's image. From their arguments, two major positive values can be discerned: "personal fulfillment" (often closely linked with women's rights) and "quality of life."

Both of these are legitimate concerns. But for the Christian, they cannot be absolute. In any event, both "fulfillment" and "quality" are relative terms. In practice, their meanings vary from person to person. One man's fulfillment may be another's frustration and one person's quality may seem cheap or meaningless to another. Life is an absolute. Where life is at stake, it is very dangerous to downgrade it, cheapen it, or destroy it for the sake of relative values such as "fulfillment" and "quality." These secondary values usually can be protected without destroying life; where this is absolutely impossible, they must take second place.

Many of the arguments for abortion are *utilitarian*. The arrival of a new child would burden an unmarried mother, a family that is already too large, or even society's welfare budget. All this may be true, but the trouble with a utilitarian way of thinking, which holds that a person's value must be weighed in terms of his usefulness, is that in the last analysis "anything goes." Anything goes if it can be shown to be useful to a majority. Tyrannical governments and dictatorships of all kinds have always tried to maintain power by exploiting some for the benefit of others.

The abortion system, then, consciously or unconsciously converts people from the "Hippocratic" ethic (which is essentially the Judaeo-Christian ethic) of the value of all human life to a utilitarian ethic that values life in terms of its convenience, usefulness, and cost. An unwanted baby is inconvenient, expensive, and not useful at all. With a utilitarian ethic there is no reason to protect it. Since *Roe* v. *Wade,* an unborn child in America has no protection.

Does this mean we have made utilitarianism into "the law of the land"? No—not consciously or deliberately. But if abortion is converting hundreds of thousands to practical utilitarianism today, what will those same thousands do when another group decides they have outlived their usefulness?

According to statistics, we are terminating "safely and legally" at least one in four new pregnancies in America before birth. What will the survivors say forty years from now when the parents who aborted their brothers and sisters are old, decrepit, and expensive to support?

According to Euripedes, "Whom the gods would destroy, they first make mad [insane]." The apostle Paul, speaking with the inspiration of the Holy Spirit, put it a little differently: "Professing to be wise, they became fools" (Rom. 1:22). Isn't it a little foolish for today's healthy, vigorous young people to destroy a quarter of the incoming generation for their own convenience, fulfillment, or even "quality of life"? But some people think it is wisdom. What kind of society does such wisdom produce?

3

Our Brave New World?

Unless the LORD build the house, they labor in vain who build it.

—Psalm 127:1

Clearly those who promote abortion do so because they think it does good to individuals and ultimately to society. Unwanted children are a burden, a social problem, and perhaps even a menace. A number of writers have tried to show that unwanted children suffer more and cause more trouble than "wanted" ones. (Much has been said for and against this theory, but it is hard to see how any clear statistics could be developed since the data are so subjective.) Whether or not this theory is true, those who support abortion clearly think that in so doing they are helping to build a better world. Usually they want to promote the "quality of life."

America is not the first society to experiment with "abortion on demand." Some countries have been involved in it for a number of years. By now they have been able to gain some experience about its impact on people and on society as a whole. Two regions of the world where abortion on demand, or something close to it, has been instituted are the Communist nations and Japan. In both cases, they have an experience of abortion that goes back twenty years or more. Are they satisfied with the results? Evidently not, for their laws and practices are being tightened.

DEATH BEFORE BIRTH

The "Benefits" of Easy Abortion

What are the benefits expected from a policy of easy abortion such as we now have in the United States? They can be divided into three categories: (1) benefits to the woman seeking an abortion, (2) benefits to particular social institutions (welfare services, etc.), and (3) benefits to the general population.

Abortion is generally advocated because of its supposed benefits to women. But once it is legalized, it is often defended on the basis of its necessity to social institutions or even to the general population. For example, Senator Charles Percy (R., Ill.) has defended abortion on the Senate floor on the grounds that it saves the state of Illinois and its taxpayers tremendous sums of money every year.[1] When something is started supposedly for one reason (the sake of the women in distress), but then is defended for other reasons, it may be a clue to the fact that the original benefits are not materializing. Let us ask, then, how women are faring with easy abortion.

Safely (?) and Legally

One of the fundamental arguments for legal abortion in every Western society where it has been advocated has been that it is necessary to cut down on illegal abortions, which supposedly took a tremendous toll in women's lives each year. The number of illegal abortions performed each year was impossible to document with any accuracy because, since abortions were illegal, they were not reported. But very high figures were cited. In the pro-abortion campaign in France, for example, it was charged that they ran as high as 500,000 per year.[2] It was often alleged that over 1 million illegal abortions were being performed annually in the United States prior to legalization. And of course illegal abortions are highly dangerous, supposedly producing countless casualties each year.

---

[1]See *Congressional Record*, May 27, 1975.
[2]*L'Avortement Histoire d'un débat* (Paris: Flammarion, 1975), pp. 178–79.

OUR BRAVE NEW WORLD?

There is no doubt that an abortion is a major surgical procedure. When performed by well-qualified personnel under excellent hospital conditions, an abortion, like any other operation, always has *some* danger. It stands to reason that abortions performed under "back-alley" conditions by ill-qualified people or even by women on themselves will be far more dangerous. Pro-abortion activists paraded around the halls of Congress when the Hyde Amendment (cutting off federal funds for "elective" abortions) was being voted on in October, 1976, carrying straightened wire coat hangers—the symbol of the self-performed abortion.

Nevertheless, a body is hard to hide, even in violence-prone America. If there were a high degree of fatalities from illegal abortions, there would also be many bodies to account for. For every dead body, there would have to be a death certificate that normally would give a strong clue to a botched abortion as the cause of death. Although estimates of very high death tolls were widely voiced—perhaps 10,000 per year in America alone—the highest number that could be *documented* was between one and two hundred deaths annually. *If* the large number of illegal abortions claimed were actually being performed, then, as Georgetown University medical professor Dr. André Hellegers said, illegal abortion would be shown to be the safest of all medical procedures—far safer than legal abortion, where there is always a certain number of fatalities, however slight.

How can we reconcile the very low rate of illegal abortion fatalities prior to 1973 with the claims that hundreds of thousands of women were resorting to illegal abortions each year? There are two possibilities. First, the actual number of illegal abortions must have been much lower than claimed. Otherwise, the number of abortion fatalities would have been much higher than it was. Second, many of the so-called "back-alley" abortions were really just "back-door" abortions, performed by competent physicians in properly-equipped facilities. The patient simply went in by the back door and the real nature of her operation was covered up.

45

Legal abortions have soared to above 1 million per year. If illegal abortions had been anywhere near that high prior to 1973, then legalization should not have had a drastic effect on the birth rate and on the number of babies available for adoption. All social workers, adoption counselors, and would-be adoptive parents know, however, that since 1970—the year New York's legalization of abortion began to have an impact—the availability of adoptive newborns has virtually dried up.

There can be no doubt that some of the women who obtain legal abortions today would obtain illegal ones if the former were not available. But there can be no doubt that the majority of today's legal abortions are performed on women who would have found some other way of dealing with the problem if abortion were still illegal. Many of the "unwanted" children would have been born and large numbers of them would have come to be wanted and loved.

How many readers of these pages can be sure their mothers *wanted* them at the time they were conceived and all through their pregnancy? Probably quite a few of us who were born during the Depression or the difficult war years would not be around today if abortion on demand had been the rule, or even encouraged by government and the media.

What does all this mean? It means that when talking of the "benefits" of legal abortion for women, we must bear in mind that many more women now have this "safe, legal" operation than would be the case if abortion were illegal. And no surgical operation is altogether trouble-free.

Furthermore, although society has to consider the implications of attempting to forbid something that people are going to do anyway, we should not embrace the general principle that whatever people will do should be legalized.

The Example of Prohibition

The failure of Prohibition is usually cited as an argument in favor of the legalization of abortion (and of some other things, such as marijuana). There is a certain logic in saying that if a particular behavior cannot effectively be stopped, forbidding it only encourages people to break the law. On the other hand, to accept this as a principle would clearly make a mockery of the whole law.

Murder, apparently, cannot be stopped in the United States. We have thousands of murders annually; some major cities frequently report several violent murders in one twenty-four-hour period. Yet no one suggests that since people are going to kill anyway, murder should be "decriminalized." Quite the contrary: a tremendous effort is being made nationwide to limit or eliminate individual possession of handguns.

The same argument pro-abortionists use against anti-abortion legislation is being used by opponents of gun control: "When gun ownership is made a crime, only criminals will still have guns." Of course, both arguments are right—but irrelevant. If abortion is once again made a crime, then only criminals—by definition—will perform abortions.

But obviously something more is at stake here than the mere question of definition. What is at stake is whether society as a whole can tolerate a certain practice—be it the use of alcoholic beverages, abortion on demand, pornography, or handgun possession. To understand the merits of the arguments for and against abortion, we need to look at the facts of the case, not at a slogan.[3]

---

[3]The same principle applies to other questions as well. When the general public is urged to vote for or against a law that involves a question of *principle,* as each of these issues does, it is intellectually dishonest and a denial of the basic principles of democracy to use slogans instead of presenting facts and logical arguments. If "rule by slogan" continues to be the way major issues are settled in America, we won't need to abolish democracy; it will have become a dead letter. Grouping these four issues together—alcohol, abortion, pornography, and handgun control—does not mean they are equally important, nor even that we should necessarily be equally opposed to or in favor of all of them. But they all have this in common: each has serious implications for the future of society, and each is more often discussed with slogans than with meaningful facts and logical arguments.

DEATH BEFORE BIRTH

A Government "Bill of Health"

It isn't at all evident that just as many women would have illegal abortions as now have legal ones if abortions were again made hard to obtain. It also wasn't certain that the total number of abortion-related maternal deaths would drop significantly with legalized abortion since, as we have seen, it was in fact very low even before legalization. But what *is* evident is that more American women than ever before are being subjected to this "safe, legal" procedure. What impact does it have on them, their physical health, their psychological stability, and their future children?

As far as the official position of the U.S. government is concerned, elective abortion is not only legal, but medically safe and problem-free. *Legalized Abortion and the Public Health,* produced in May of 1975 by the National Institute of Health (NIH), virtually gives the abortion procedure a clean bill of health. The report's most eminent sponsor, Dean Frederick C. Robbins, M.D., of Case-Western Reserve Medical School, commented in a press conference at the time of publication that the report would be unwelcome among anti-abortionists, but that it was the duty of scientists to present the facts. But did the report actually present the facts?

Shortly after publication, Dr. Robbins was challenged on the grounds that to give a questionable medical procedure such a thorough whitewashing when there is so much evidence of serious complications is unethical. Dr. Robbins repudiated the suggestion of unethical conduct. He was, however, unwilling to say he would dissociate himself from the report if sound evidence were presented to show its inaccuracy.[4] Dr. André Hellegers of Georgetown's Kennedy Institute, one of the world's outstanding authorities on medical ethics, has said the entire

---

[4]Unpublished correspondence between Dr. Robbins and the writer.

report is a whitewash of abortion, put together by a one-sided pro-abortion group, and is basically unreliable.[5]

The strange thing about *Legalized Abortion and the Public Health* is that it was published four months after the Fourth International Conference on Perinatal Medicine in Prague, Czechoslovakia, in which Professor Alfred Kotásek reported in detail on almost 2 million abortions performed in his country over a twenty-year period. Kotásek's findings revealed a high degree of complications following abortions, particularly when they are abortions of the first pregnancy. Since Czechoslovakia allows elective abortions only during the first twelve weeks of pregnancy, *all* the abortions on which Kotásek reported were early abortions. It is precisely the early abortions that *Legalized Abortion* states to be for all practical purposes trouble-free.

In light of the panic into which government health authorities fly and the excitement they cause whenever they discover an apparent link between any currently available product and cancer or other serious disease, it really is remarkable that the NIH study completely glosses over all the evidence from Europe concerning the problems resulting from early abortions.

Suppose hundreds of thousands of men each year contracted a venereal disease.[6] An operation was widely recommended as a safe, easy cure. In early 1975, by which time 1 million such operations per year were being performed, a major European medical congress stated that as many as one-fourth of all men having the operation would encounter serious difficulty ever becoming the father of a normal child. And suppose the NIH

[5]This information comes from personal conversation between Dr. Hellegers and the writer.

[6]Apparently HEW considers pregnancy a veneral disease. This was the position taken by Dr. Willard Cates, Jr., Chief of the Abortion Surveillance Branch of the Family Planning Evaluation Division, Bureau of Epidemiology, Center for Disease Control, Public Health Service, Department of Health, Education, and Welfare, in a widely publicized letter of January 4, 1977, to John P. Mackey, Esq. of the Ad Hoc Committee in Defense of Life.

simply dismissed it out of hand instead of dealing with the European evidence.

We could expect two things to happen. First, the medical problem would gradually begin to show up and there would be a great number of unhappy men and troubled marriages. Second, any physicians and government officials who had taken part in the cover-up would come in for some very harsh criticism.

This offers a fairly close parallel to what is going on with abortion—even to saying that, as far as HEW is concerned, unwanted pregnancy is a venereal disease. Of course, for those who look at the derivation of words, pregnancy does involve a certain indisposition (dis-ease), and it is *venereal* in origin (from Venus, goddess of love).

However, I think most ordinary English speakers will become a little uneasy at the description of pregnancy—one's own mother's pregnancy could also be so described—as a "venereal disease" to be dealt with by the Center for Disease Control, with abortion as the prescribed "treatment." Isn't this dangerously close to George Orwell's world of *Nineteen Eighty-Four,* where the secret police are run by the "Ministry of Love"? Admittedly, all bureaucratese is a strange language, but this particular bureaucratese looks frighteningly like Orwell's Newspeak.

In any event, the positions are clear. As far as HEW is concerned, unwanted pregnancy is a disease for which abortion is a relatively harmless treatment. (The new Secretary of HEW, Joseph A. Califano, is on record as being *opposed* to abortion, and this is greatly to his credit.) The official HEW position is shared by the abortion clinics and the "pregnancy counseling" or "abortion referral" services. Since most major newspapers run advertisements for such "services," any interested reader can easily check this out. If you are a woman of childbearing age, call and ask what to do about an unwanted pregnancy. When advised to have an abortion, query the "service" about the reports from Poland, Czechoslovakia, Germany, and Britain on the danger of early abortions.[7] Individual physicians, if they are responsible, will answer questions about the dangers of abortion, but of course they too may be misled by impressive-appearing publications such as *Legalized Abortion and the Public Health.*

The Complications

In its 1975 law which permits abortion during the first ten weeks of pregnancy, France requires that a woman seeking an abortion be advised by her physician of possible dangers to herself and to her future prospects of motherhood. The woman must sign a form indicating she has been so advised. This is a far cry from the American situation in which the government, contrary to much evidence, continues to assure women there is no danger involved.

It is also clear evidence of the fact that in influential government circles population reduction is such a priority goal that almost any means that promotes it is acceptable. After all, if a girl who has an early abortion later discovers she can no longer give birth, so much the better. It's another step on the road to negative population growth.

As indicated by a number of studies, the chief danger in early abortion is to the young woman who has never given birth.[8] The biggest problem such a woman faces is the possibility that, as a

[7]Several of my students at Trinity Evangelical Divinity School called a number of abortion services in the Midwest and posed this question. Without exception the dangers were pooh-poohed. The students were told that Poles and Czechs could not be compared to American women (why not?), that the techniques aren't the same (they are), or that Europeans do not have sanitary operating conditions (they do). Of course, these "services" have a financial interest in not alarming potential clients. The interest of HEW, which is just asking for trouble in the future due to all the complications, is harder to understand.

[8]Technical medical papers on the subject have been prepared by a number of specialists, foremost among them Professor Alfred Kotásek, M.D., D.Sc., whose essay, "Medical Complications of Induced Abortion," is reprinted in the *Human Life Review*, Vol. 1:4 (Fall, 1975). See also Stanisław Lembrych, M.D., "The Course of Pregnancy, Birth, and Lying-In After the Artificial Termination of the First Pregnancy," *Human Life Review*, Vol. 1:3 (Summer, 1975).

result of having her first pregnancy aborted, she will find it difficult or even impossible to carry a second pregnancy to term. The cause of her possible difficulty is easy to understand, even for those without specific medical knowledge.

In a young woman who has never been pregnant, the uterus or womb is a very small organ, no larger than a medium-sized potato. In a pregnant woman, the uterus grows with the developing fetus until, just before birth, its dimensions are as large as necessary to contain the fully formed baby. The cervix, or neck of the womb, is surrounded by muscles which also develop and become stronger as the baby grows. It is their task to support the baby and keep it properly within the uterus until the time for delivery comes.

In an early abortion, whether by the older "D & C" (dilatation and curettage) or the more modern "vacuum aspiration" (sometimes called a suction D & C), the physician must expand the cervix to perform the operation. He does this by inserting a series of rings or tubes of gradually increasing diameter. These spread the muscles apart and keep the neck of the womb open for the insertion of the curette or vacuum apparatus and the removal of the "fetal remains."

Because the uterus is immature, the cervical muscles are not fully strengthened and there is considerable chance they will be permanently weakened by the forcible dilatation. When this happens and the woman subsequently becomes pregnant with a wanted baby, the weakened muscles may not be able to hold in the developing baby. They may give way, resulting in premature labor and what might be a "spontaneous mid-term abortion." Where they have been less seriously affected, the premature labor may come on later, resulting in a live but premature baby. However, since premature infants are more likely than full-term babies to suffer from various birth defects, the risk of prematurity is also a factor that should be considered, as well as the more serious possibility of spontaneous abortions of the second and later pregnancies.

An abortion of a second or later pregnancy, performed after a

fully-developed baby has been born, does not involve this particular risk. On the other hand, when not only the first pregnancy but the second and subsequent pregnancies are deliberately aborted, the chances of ever having a normal delivery
decrease.

In the Chicago area, abortion services were advising callers as
late as the fall of 1976 that "up to four" pregnancies could be
aborted by this method with no serious danger. In view of the
fact that Professor Kotásek discovered a complication rate ap-
proaching twenty-five percent in early abortions, one might
suspect that four early abortions in succession would make a
woman almost certain to have serious trouble with a wanted
pregnancy. Of course, we cannot simply multiply probabilities;
the weakened cervical muscles would yield more easily to dilatation in the later abortions and hence subsequent damage might
well be less than that from the initial abortion. However, it is
perfectly clear that each fresh assault on an organ increases the
likelihood of subsequent problems.

Psychiatric Complications

In his major study, Professor Kotásek does not deal with
psychological, psychosexual, emotional, and other non-
physiological complications of abortions, although he points out
they exist and are substantial. It is very difficult to obtain a
comprehensive view of possible psychiatric complications of
abortion because most abortion services do not maintain
follow-up surveillance of patients. In any event, it is difficult to
tell what caused a psychiatric problem without a thorough
psychiatric examination.

It is very easy to see how such psychiatric problems arise. First
of all, the Western world has held for 2,500 years that abortion
is morally wrong. It is true that abortion has been practiced,
particularly in pagan antiquity. But even many pagans who were
advocates of sexual liberty—such as the Roman poet Ovid—
condemned abortion as murder. With the establishment of the

Hippocratic Oath and the rise of Christianity, it came to be generally accepted that abortion is an atrocious crime.

Orthodox Judaism, Roman Catholicism, and biblical Protestantism—which together include the majority of America's people—all teach that abortion is a very serious attack on a human being made in the image of God, and is a grievous sin. This also holds true for other religions such as Mormonism. It stands to reason that any woman from one of these traditions— and this would include the majority of American women—is going to have problems with guilt over an abortion.

Despite several decades of propaganda and general public tolerance in the area of sexual "liberty" (better called "license"), today's men and women often find themselves burdened with guilt feelings and psychological problems as a result of sexual misconduct, even though they tell themselves and others that they believe their conduct is perfectly justifiable. In the case where such misconduct is not just a "one-night stand," but results in the death of a developing child through abortion, it stands to reason that a large number of women would have serious problems with unresolved guilt. And contrary to popular thought, they do not need to be connected with a Christian church to have that problem of guilt. The belief that abortion is wrong is so much a part of our culture that it will almost inevitably affect any woman who has one, regardless of what she thinks she believes about the morality of abortion.

Speaking strictly from a professional and common-sense viewpoint, a female Indian gynecologist confessed that she herself was deeply shaken by every abortion, even though she believed it was both legal and acceptable. If I am so deeply affected, the worker wondered, how can the woman who has carried the child within her own body for five months not be *more* affected?[9]

Dr. C. Everett Koop of Philadelphia has dealt with several thousand severely handicapped children and their parents over a thirty-year period. He tells of the overwhelming guilt feelings

[9]Denes, *In Necessity and Sorrow,* p. 72.

many parents of handicapped children experience even though they are in no way responsible for the problems of their child. If parents who have done nothing to harm a child feel terribly guilty when they have a handicapped child, what will happen to the woman whose first live child is born handicapped after she has had an abortion? And what about the woman who wants a child but cannot have one? Won't she suspect it may have something to do with her earlier abortion? What about the man who wants a child but whose wife cannot bear one because she had an abortion, either of another man's child or of his own?

Studies of the psychological complications of abortion deal almost exclusively with the *women* involved. But as the previous question suggests, it would be ridiculous to overlook the fact that more than one adult is involved in an abortion. Just as there can be no conception without two persons involved, there are always several adults or adolescents involved in an abortion: the woman, the man who fathered the child, and at least one physician. No physician is ever *forced* to perform an abortion. (Supposedly, no nurse or other medical personnel is either, but frequently so much pressure exists that for all practical purposes staff members *are* forced.) Therefore, we might assume that all physicians do so of their own free will and hence should be free of qualms. Unfortunately, as the "dean" (if we may call him such) of abortion physicians in America, Bernard N. Nathanson, testifies, abortionists and their supporting staffs often have terrible recurring guilt feelings, nightmares, and other problems as a result of their activities.[10] The serious problem of what abortion does to the medical profession and to others in health care is one that needs to be seriously faced and considered.

The Man's Role

But let us leave the question of the doctors, nurses, and others actively involved and turn to the one who seems even more

---

[10]Bernard N. Nathanson, "Deeper into Abortion," *New England Journal of Medicine*, Vol. 291:22 (Nov. 28, 1974), pp. 1189–90.

passive than the woman—the father of the unborn child. Again Dr. Denes offers some insights. Men are very uncomfortable around the abortion hospital, she reports. They cannot deny the fact that it is they who have gotten the women into trouble—or, if we prefer to avoid such old-fashioned language, in for what Associate Justice Douglas called a "distressful future." Of course, many a man just leaves his sex partner on her own to deal with the "product of conception." Sometimes the man never even finds out that the girl with whom he had sexual relations has become pregnant. The majority, apparently, are aware of the girl's problem and do consent to the abortion; perhaps they recommend it, encourage it, or even pay for it. But their participation stops at the door of the operating room, if not at the door of the clinic itself.

Any surgical operation is to some extent a frightening, humiliating procedure. The patient, like a sacrificial victim, is unclothed and examined by a number of impersonal observers. By submitting to the anesthesia, he is deprived even of conscious awareness of what is happening to him and he puts himself entirely into the hands of others. The recovery too leaves him with a feeling of vulnerability, weakness, and even helplessness.

Modern medicine has done much to remove the anxiety from surgical operations. A tremendous academic and professional establishment has been built up to assure the competence and reliability of the operating personnel. Twenty-five hundred years of medical history assure the patient—or did until recently—that the doctor's first responsibility is to do no harm and that he can be trusted to act in his patient's best interest.

Abortion is a surgical operation with some special features. First, although the patient is in a sense the victim, she is aware that she also *has* a victim—the little being whose life is being snuffed out at her request. Thus not only does she feel threatened, she must also have at least certain twinges of guilt. There is joy amidst the pain in a hospital when an operation is successful and the patient, relatives, and staff can look forward to recovery. There can't be anything like the same sense of fulfillment and joy when an abortion is "successfully" completed. Magda Denes likens the corpses she saw awaiting disposal in her abortion hospital to slain soldiers seen lying on a battlefield and comments, "A death factory is the same anywhere; the agony of early death is the same anywhere."[11] In a way, we can rejoice at the brutal honesty that is emerging among the pro-abortionists. Some, like Magda Denes, appear tormented by what they know, and her readers will almost surely share some of her sense of horror. But there is one unfortunate aspect to this present honesty. Pro-abortionists persuaded many to accept their views by claiming that no killing is involved because the fetus isn't yet human. Today many of them are totally frank about what goes on in an abortion. The frightening thing is that in four short years abortion has become so much a way of life in America that now the truth can safely be told and people no longer get disturbed by it.

The psychological deadening of ordinary human emotions in the abortion issue is similar to what takes place in a war. But in war there is a life-and-death situation, with two enemies locked in mortal conflict and perpetrating atrocities on each other. Who is the enemy in abortion? All the atrocities are on one side. It begins to look as though the present adult generation regards future humanity as its enemy, for whom no fate is too severe. How will the survivors of this present generation of babies and unborn children feel toward the adults who looked on them as the enemy? There is a grim plausibility in a headline from *New Statesman:* "The Abortion Wave of the '60s Will Be the Euthanasia Wave of the '80s."

More Facts Needed?

It is evident that an abortion, far from being trouble-free, carries with it considerable risk of physical complications. This risk is especially high when the first pregnancy is being aborted

---

[11]Denes, *In Necessity and Sorrow,* p. 60.

and when the woman subsequently seeks to have a child. This is why French law requires a signed statement from a woman seeking an abortion to the effect that she has been made aware of the risks. In Communist Eastern Europe, where easy abortions have been the rule for twenty years, it is precisely the most advanced countries that are trying to restrict them as much as possible.

A state-run health system cannot knowingly advise operations that are likely to confront it with an epidemic of problems within a few years (e.g., defective babies, sterility, psychological problems). The largely private abortion business in the United States has no such qualms, of course, for when problems develop here, the abortion facilities won't have to deal with them—or pay for them. So our money-making clinics promote abortions while the Eastern Europeans are doing all they can to discourage them.

As far as psychological damage goes, there is no hard evidence. It will take considerable follow-up and much research to show beyond all reasonable doubt that abortion "may be dangerous to your mental health." That follow-up and research will probably be a long time coming because the source of funds for most such research is either the government or one of the major foundations.

How much impartiality can we expect from the government? If *Legalized Abortion and the Public Health* is any indication, we can't expect our government to put out a balanced study on the psychological aspects of abortion until the problems have begun to come home with a vengeance, as they have in Czechoslovakia and Poland.

More than one of the great foundations, following the lead of the Rockefeller group, have put a great deal of money into pro-abortion research. The Playboy Foundation provided grants to finance the historical "studies" that formed the groundwork of the Supreme Court's *Roe* v. *Wade* decision. And of course the abortionists and their facilities have plenty of money—perhaps one third of it directly provided by the government—and they are willing to make generous contributions to stay in business, but not necessarily to fund studies that might show they should be put out of business.

Hard facts indicating the psychological dangers of abortion will probably be a long time coming, given the evident bias of both government and many foundations. In a way, this bias is easy to understand. No one usually makes money when an unwanted child is allowed to be born (except in the case of black-market babies sold to adoptive parents who can find one nowhere else). An "unwanted" child costs everyone involved something. The pregnant woman is involved in loss of time, physical discomfort, and emotional strain. Someone must provide and pay for medical care, delivery, and infancy expense. And it will be many years before such an unwanted child joins the army of producers and begins to pay taxes.

On the other hand, everybody—or so it would seem—profits from an abortion. The woman's time loss is cut and her discomfort may be less, or at least less drawn out. A doctor makes a good fee from a few minutes' work with no follow-up responsibilities. (How many women want their abortionists to become their regular physicians?) And the abortion facility and the associated services all make money. So do government officials such as Dr. Willard Cates of the Abortion Surveillance Branch, as he surveys success in "treating" what he calls a "sexually transmitted condition," and what ordinary human language calls a developing baby.

Nobody profits from an unwanted baby; quite a few people "profit" from the abortion business. Unfortunately, what is true of unwanted babies is also true of those who are wanted. They cost their mothers and fathers loss of time, as well as discomfort, care, and expense. Prenatal, delivery, and postnatal care is more time-consuming for an obstetrician than is an abortion and brings proportionately less revenue for the time and effort involved.

Births—except for Caesarean sections and induced labor—

can't be scheduled. An abortionist can work a forty-hour week if he chooses, and get rich. Ordinary obstetricians have to be available when their patients' babies are ready for them.

The government has to provide services—schools, public health, and sometimes welfare services—for wanted babies as well as for unwanted ones. And it takes a wanted baby just about as long to grow up and start paying taxes as it does an unwanted one—perhaps even longer, since a wanted child's parents may be more likely to send him to college, thus increasing further still the child's "cost" and delaying the point at which he begins to start paying the state back in taxes for the privilege of being allowed to be born.

The arguments showing how practical, useful, and economical abortion of unwanted pregnancies is, unfortunately also work to show how expensive and burdensome even *wanted* children are. This is part of the explanation for the drastic drop in the overall birth rate. Human beings, since time began, have realized that children are a lot of trouble, but generally they have considered them to be worth the effort. Our society tells us, by supporting abortion on demand, that children are *not* worth the trouble. Logically, that applies to wanted children as well as to unwanted ones, and so the result is that fewer and fewer children are being wanted. Through contraception, fewer children are conceived. Thanks to abortion, fewer of those conceived are being born. And then, paradoxically, more of those being born turn out to be "battered children"—the victims of child abuse.

Child Abuse

Among the probable results of easy abortion we must list the rapidly growing problem of child abuse, which has reached almost epidemic proportions. Child abuse includes physical assault; recently, attention has been drawn specifically to the sexual abuse of children. More and more frequently, one hears of children being used for pornographic purposes. Legislation is currently pending in Illinois and elsewhere which would forbid the use of children in pornography.

Child abuse was one of the arguments used in favor of abortion. In fact, in congressional debates on the subject, one still hears the argument that an unwanted child is more likely than a wanted child to become the victim of abuse. Hence it is supposed to be kinder to the unwanted child to abort it than to allow it to be born and possibly suffer mistreatment. (Here we have a principle that goes too far—rather like the suggestion that a person who is afraid of being mugged can protect himself by suicide.)

The pro-abortionists have had their way. Since 1970, we can conservatively estimate that there are 5 million fewer children between the ages of one and seven in America than there would be if we had not legalized abortion. Since these 5 million were the "unwanted" who supposedly would have been the prime targets for child abuse, it would seem reasonable to look for a remarkable drop in child abuse in the same period. It may seem reasonable, but it hasn't happened. Since abortion on demand, reported child abuse has grown to virtually epidemic proportions. (See Appendix, p. 165.) This might not represent a direct cause-and-effect relationship, but it is a fact.

If abortion eliminates "unwanted" children, then who is being battered and abused? The answer lies in two errors involved in the assumption that since "unwanted" babies are the likelier candidates for abuse and abortion gets rid of them, abuse will drop as abortions increase.

The first error lies in dividing babies into the categories of "wanted" and "unwanted." Few babies are totally "wanted" at every point during their mother's pregnancy, but quite a few "unwanted" babies become wanted when they actually make their appearance, however unwelcome they seemed beforehand. On the other hand, many babies that were thoroughly wanted become burdens and nuisances to parents after birth.

The second error lies in the failure to recognize what we

61

might call the "educational impact" of nationwide abortion on demand. The West German Federal Constitutional Court (Supreme Court), in its February, 1975, decision banning abortion on demand during the first twelve weeks of pregnancy (as passed by the *Bundestag*) stated, "We cannot ignore the educational impact of abortion on the respect for life." The German court reasoned that if abortion were made legal for any and every reason during the first trimester, it would prove hard to persuade people that the second- and third-trimester fetus deserves protection simply by virtue of having grown a few weeks older.

Apparently, what the West German court feared would happen to late fetuses also happens to children after birth. Parents, perhaps unconsciously, may reason, "I didn't have to have him. I could have killed him before he was born. So if I knock him around a little now that he is born, isn't that my perfect right?"

It is unlikely that anyone actually reasons that way in a conscious sense, but some such unconscious rationalization must be taking place. After all, if one can legally kill the child a few months before birth, what can be so bad about roughing him up a little without killing him? Many parents who are burdened with their children must feel resentment at not having taken advantage of the opportunity to abort them; thus, they take it out on them after birth.

Among the psychological and psychiatric complications of abortion, then, we must include the increase in the number of battered children as well as the rise in the mentality that considers children a burden and caring for them an unreasonable chore. Where will such a mentality lead us? Clearly, right to a population crisis—but of a different kind from the one so many have been predicting. It will lead to a drastically declining population. If we think the "population explosion" threatens the "quality of life," we ought to take a good look at the impact of the birth dearth.

OUR BRAVE NEW WORLD?

Poland Is Not Yet Lost

During one hundred and twenty years of being overrun by Germans, Russians, and Austrians, the Polish people sang their anthem, *Polska jeszcze nie zgniela,* "Poland Is Not Yet Lost." But a noted Polish professor of pediatrics in Cracow recently commented to an American visitor: "Our abortion policies were bringing us to the brink of national genocide." And so Poland, as well as several other Eastern European countries and the Soviet Union, is severely cutting back on its easy abortion policies. The reason is simple. Poland may not yet be lost, but without a healthy generation of young Poles it soon will be.

No reasonable person will deny that unchecked population growth is a problem. It is evident that any particular nation and the earth itself have limits to the number of people they can support. However, it is possible to err in more than one direction.

Japan, crushed, humiliated, and crowded back into the home islands after her defeat in World War II, saw drastic population control as the only way to get through the crisis. Thus Japan resorted to abortion on an unprecedented scale. Abortion on demand is not the law in Japan; there are fairly severe restrictions on paper. But in practice there are no controls. Since the late 1940s, perhaps as many as 50 million abortions have been performed in the island empire.

As a result, the dynamic Japan of the late 1950s and 1960s now sees itself with an aging population and a labor shortage. Approximately 10 million Korean workers have been admitted into Japan to keep Japanese industry going. A similar situation prevails in several industrialized European nations, where the birth rate has been falling even without abortion on demand. Germany and Switzerland, and to a lesser extent France, have to import "guest labor"—southern Europeans, North Africans, and Turks—to work in the factories, hotels, and service operations that cannot be staffed by nationals.

Indeed, the United States faces a similar situation, although it is usually not admitted as such. It is estimated that there are almost 10 million illegal immigrants in this country. Since true unemployment is less than that, it is fair to assume that at least some of that illegal immigration is "necessary" to do work for which there are no native-born Americans available.

A New Black Death?

Countries such as Poland, Hungary, Czechoslovakia, and the Soviet Union have begun to face up to the long-range problems caused by population stagnation or even decline. France, which discouraged population growth in the nineteenth century and ran into problems because of it, is very sensitive to the increased danger of population stagnation that easy abortion can cause.[12] United Nations economist Colin Clark warns that the industrialized nations of the West, if they continue their policies promoting negative population growth, will face a worse population situation by the end of this century than that caused by the Black Death during the late Middle Ages.[13]

Nowhere is this more apparent than in the whole question of retirement financing and the Social Security system. Population growth analyst James Weber writes, "Currently some 92 million workers are providing benefits to 30 million retirees—about a 3-to-1 ratio. But based on present trends, this ratio will sink to two to one by the turn of the century, a far cry from the 150-to-1 ratio between workers and beneficiaries which existed in 1940, a few years after the Social Security program was adopted."[14]

The Social Security system is no longer breaking even. In

[12]Cf. James A. Weber, *Grow or Die: The Over-Population Myth* (New Rochelle: Arlington House, 1977), p. 26.

[13]Colin Clark, "Abortion and Population Control," *Human Life Review*, Vol. 2:3 (Summer, 1976). Cf. his *Population Growth and Land Use* (London: Macmillan, 1968).

[14]Weber, *Grow or Die,* pp. 107–108.

OUR BRAVE NEW WORLD?

March, 1977, at President Carter's behest, the Senate withdrew a proposal to raise Social Security taxes by $1 billion per year. Carter's reluctance is based on his fear that increased taxes would harm the economic growth he wants. But the fact remains that the Social Security system is already paying out more than it is taking in.

The Abortion Wave of the Sixties = the Euthanasia
Wave of the Eighties

Young people of today's present generation apparently have more money to spend partly because they have fewer children to cost them money. So far, so good. But what will be the situation when today's numerous young adults are tomorrow's numerous old retired people, and today's relatively few children are tomorrow's relatively few producers? It stands to reason that when there are only two workers to pay for one retired adult, there is going to be increasing pressure on the government from the working taxpayers to "do something about the problem of unwanted old folks."

Today's infants will learn soon enough that their parents' generation sacrificed one in four of their brothers and sisters for personal convenience and their own "quality of life." Will they feel the need to exert themselves to prolong the lives of that parental generation when it is old and demanding, but no longer producing? Thirty years from now, being able to say you were "personally opposed" to abortion will probably not be much of an argument to keep you out of the euthanasia facility. Nor is it likely that much provision will be made for giving special consideration to those who actually had their children instead of aborting them.

It is important to note that *Roe* v. *Wade* and the developments that followed gave the pro-abortion movement more than it ever asked or expected. When euthanasia is considered in the courts, they will probably give the pro-euthanasia forces more than they are asking. Therefore it is important to know what they are asking for. There are three basic levels of euthanasia demands, just as there were three basic levels of abortion demands. The abortion demands have all been fulfilled; so far, only one euthanasia demand has been fulfilled in one state—California.

On the abortion side of the table, we can see that in just four years we have made rapid "progress" away from the standards of Christianity and the Hippocratic Oath, upheld for two millennia. We have progressed from (1) abortion permitted only when it is a genuine last resort to save a mother's life, to (2) abortion as perfectly legal, morally without question, and available to all, to (3) the present situation in which its *support* has become compulsory on all, through taxes, and when its practice is very much urged upon women by agencies that find abortion the quickest, neatest, most final solution to the problem of an unwanted pregnancy.

On the euthanasia side, we have not yet moved that far. But the precedent of abortion—from generally forbidden to state support nationwide in four years—should make us alert to the fact that things can happen fast in euthanasia matters, too.

"Passive" Euthanasia?

Euthanasia (from Greek *eu-*, "good" and *thanatos*, "death"), originally meant only providing comfort, spiritual as well as medical, to the dying. In this limited sense, euthanasia is not merely proper but altogether praiseworthy. In the 1920s, it became customary to use the word "euthanasia" to mean "mercy-killing." Mercy-killing is a direct act to end the life of a suffering person. As such, it could be *voluntary* (desired by the sick person) or *involuntary* (desired by someone else). Euthanasia in this sense is a fairly straightforward term and is easy to understand.

Unfortunately, the situation has been complicated in recent years by the introduction of the term "passive euthanasia." "Passive euthanasia" means the withholding of useless treatment from a dying person. This is a practice which is both medically and ethically justified and which has been customary with responsible physicians since the beginning of medicine. However, to call this "passive euthanasia" is very misleading because the implication is that it is very similar to outright mercy-killing, or "active euthanasia."

Although the effect is the same, there is a big difference. It is like using the expression "rape" to indicate both the situation in which a woman allows herself to be drawn into sexual intercourse with a man and that in which it is forced upon her. We could call the former "passive rape" and the latter "active rape." Although it is not likely that this terminology will become current, the confusion is no worse than that caused by the use of "passive euthanasia" to describe the morally acceptable practice of letting nature take its course.

It is not clear *why* the term "passive euthanasia" has crept into our language, but it is evident what it is doing: it facilitates the arguments for euthanasia. Glanville Williams, an outspoken advocate of active euthanasia, puts it this way: "After the individual has reached a certain age, or a certain degree of decay, medical science will hold his hand, and allow him to be carried off by natural causes. But what if these natural causes are themselves painful? Would it not be better kindness to substitute human agency?"[15]

It would be far better *not* to use the term "passive euthanasia" to mean "allowing death," for the habits of our language and culture are such that we are automatically conditioned to think that if something passive is good, then what is active is even better.

It is this "allowing to die" or "passive euthanasia" that is, for the moment, all that is considered under the California Natural Death Act and similar bills. However, since this was already legal and usual prior to the passage of these bills, we must ask whether

---

[15]Glanville Williams, " 'Mercy-Killing' Legislation—A Rejoinder," *Minnesota Law Review*, Vol. 43:1 (1958), p. 12.

they are not, consciously or unconsciously, intended as a means of preparing us for true mercy-killing, "active euthanasia."

The third level of "euthanasia" goes beyond the traditional meaning even of mercy-killing. In the past, euthanasia has referred to the acceleration of the death of persons *already dying*. (This is a similarity between what is called "passive" euthanasia and "active" or true euthanasia: both deal with people who are in the process of dying.) This final category is described by Dr. Helmut E. Ehrhardt of Marburg University, Germany, as "elimination of worthless life." It deals, for example, with Down's Syndrome (Mongoloid) patients, the mentally ill, handicapped, and others. These people are not in the process of dying and must be actively put to death. Dr. Ehrhardt, a professor of psychiatry and law, remembers Nazi Germany's experience with the elimination of life "devoid of value." First it was done by the mere withholding of nourishment (starvation), then by gassing or the injection of poisonous substances.

Although active euthanasia is not yet legal in any American state, it is in effect already widely in use, particularly with defective children—especially Mongoloids. Two New Haven physicians, Raymond S. Duff and A.G.M. Campbell, clearly consider this appropriate.[16] Much of America's medical community is willing to go along with them, if not actively to endorse their views and imitate their practice.

Loyola University pediatrics professor Eugene F. Diamond points out what is happening here. No one, yet, would think of killing a newborn infant because it has Down's Syndrome. However, Down's Syndrome is often associated with duodenal atresia (intestinal blockage). This blockage prevents the child from absorbing food and, if untreated, will cause death in a matter of days or weeks. It is usually fairly easy to treat by a

---

[16]Raymond S. Duff, M.D., and A.G.M. Campbell, M.D., F.R.C.P. (Edin.), *"Moral and Ethical Dilemmas in the Special-Care Nursery,"* New England Journal of Medicine, Vol. 289:17 (1973), pp. 890–894, reprinted in *Death, Dying, and Euthanasia;* see fn. 17 below.

surgical operation. No one could think of allowing a normal infant or child to die simply because of a treatable intestinal obstruction. However, where Down's Syndrome is associated with an obstruction, it is now becoming more and more common to let the child die of starvation. This is not "passive euthanasia"; it is killing.

Do we see what is happening? One handicap—Down's Syndrome—is not enough to justify death, by starvation or any other means. Neither is another handicap, duodenal atresia. But the presence of *two* defects is enough to bring a sentence of death by starvation.[17] It will not be long before "humane" voices will be raised saying, "Since the child is going to die of starvation anyway, would it not be more humane to kill him quickly, swiftly, and painlessly?"

Most of the euthanasia discussion centers, for the moment, on "hopeless" cases. The same was true in the early days of the abortion movement and it still happens when the rightness of abortion is questioned. The cases cited are those of terrible desperation—the young teen-ager raped by an escapee from an insane asylum, for example. Abortion on demand was supposed to be required to relieve such cases of terrible necessity.

But as it turns out, we have approximately 1 million abortions per year in the United States. Do we have so many desperate cases? And where were they all before abortion was legalized in 1973? Magda Denes says that *every* abortion, by definition, is a case of "absolute necessity." But I think most Americans recognize that nearly all of our nation's million abortions each year are truly elective—not in any sense necessary, but desired for reasons of varying seriousness.

Euthanasia is desired for the "hopeless" cases. And it would be callous to ignore the fact that there are many such cases. But to allow them to be killed because a verdict has been passed on

[17]Eugene F. Diamond, M.D., "The Deformed Child's Right to Life," *Death, Dying, and Euthanasia,* Dennis J. Horan and David Mall, eds. (Washington: University Publications, 1977).

their hopelessness will clearly open the door to a very flexible interpretation of hopelessness and worthlessness, just as the admission of "psychiatric indications" for abortion in the days before *Roe* v. *Wade* opened the door for a very loose definition of mental health.

In regard to the genuinely "hopeless" cases, it would be far better for society to do what it can to share the burden of those caring for the hopeless than to eliminate the hopeless. Such sharing is far more expensive and time-consuming. However, if we accept the principle that we may relieve ourselves of expensive, time-consuming problems by eliminating the individuals who cause them, we will certainly be letting ourselves in for more than most people want to accept. For example, the arguments against capital punishment would vanish. In fact, we could replace the whole prison system with a few execution facilities! There might be some mistakes, of course, but society would save a lot of money.[18]

If any form of euthanasia is legitimized for so-called hopeless cases—and it is already being practiced, although not yet legalized—it will not be long before we move from the "hopeless" to the merely "valueless." Most Mongoloids, for example—one of the primary targets of current euthanasia practices—are not "hopeless." They can have useful and productive lives. Down's Syndrome children are traditionally known as "happy babies," perhaps because their limited intelligence, with IQs running from 30 to 90, keeps them from understanding just how bad the world is!

---

[18]Perhaps a personal note is in order here. During the time when California was debating its natural death bill, I visited a former high school classmate who had recently lost his wife after many years of struggle with cancer. He described in some detail her last months, when she was enfeebled, in much pain, and almost completely helpless, and how hard this was on her and on their children. I was expecting him to say that he would have valued the possibility of mercy-killing and was wondering how to answer him, when instead he said, "But it was better for her to bear that suffering, as hard as it was, and for our family to have the grief of watching her die than it would be to pass a law enabling us to kill such cases. We have no idea where it would end."

OUR BRAVE NEW WORLD?

In Zurich, Switzerland, Mongoloid children are employed in a sheltered workshop repairing telephones (and the Swiss telephone service is as good or better than ours!). The vast majority of such children do not need to be hospitalized; they can live useful and happy lives at home. Dr. Diamond points out that even if *all* the Down's Syndrome children in the United States were hospitalized, the total cost would be only one-tenth of what our nation annually spends on dog food![19]

Because some physicians are willing to let a Down's Syndrome child die if it also has a treatable intestinal obstruction, what actually happens is that the children are left to starve. At times, even ordinary treatment such as providing water is forbidden. One surgeon describes the "suffering" he undergoes watching a salvageable baby die as "the most emotionally exhausting experience I know. It is easy at a conference, in a theoretical discussion, to decide that such infants should be allowed to die. It is altogether different to stand by in the nursery and watch as dehydration and infection wither a tiny being over hours and days. This is a terrible ordeal *for me and the hospital staff*, much more so than for the parents who never set foot in the nursery" [italics added].[20]

Dr. Diamond comments, "One would never guess from the foregoing that starvation was a terrible ordeal for the infant who is being starved. I would suggest that most Down's Syndrome children obliged to watch a surgeon starve would feel sorry for the surgeon and not for themselves."[21]

How far is this surgeon's "terrible ordeal" removed from that of the German doctors and psychiatrists who ordered the starvation deaths of retarded patients? There is a precedent for whitewashing such behavior on the part of physicians. In a postwar trial in Frankfurt, Germany, the court ruled on the case of a psychiatrist who not only killed many patients—adults and

[19]Diamond, "The Deformed Child's Right to Life," p. 129.
[20]Diamond, p. 137, citing A. Shaw, "Doctor, Do We Have a Choice?" *New York Times Magazine*, Jan. 30, 1972, p. 54.
[21]Ibid.

children—but also observed their death agonies. The court said, "We deal with a certain human weakness which does not as yet deserve moral condemnation."[22]

The Abortion Wave of the Sixties . . .

We are not yet in the eighties and not yet in the middle of the predicted euthanasia wave. But we are already in the euthanasia ripples. Amniocentesis—a procedure permitting some conditions to be diagnosed while the baby is still in the womb—has made possible the "prevention" of many birth defects by eliminating the defective baby before birth. But since these techniques are not yet universally applied, many defects are not "prevented"; that is, babies are born with defects. And the tendency is to let them die, although it is a "terrible ordeal" for the doctors and hospital personnel who have to watch. Perhaps in this climate of opinion we will soon be permitting the killing of such dying patients to spare their attendants the "terrible ordeal" of watching them die!

Perhaps the final stage in the development toward euthanasia is reflected in a bill proposed by Wisconsin legislator Lloyd A. Barbee. This bill sounds so bizarre that it is hard to believe it was seriously proposed. However, although it was defeated, apparently it *was* seriously proposed and evaluated. It provides that anyone over seven may request to be killed, and that anyone over fifteen may fulfill that request for him.[23] If the request is made by a minor, the parents must be informed, but their consent is not required. If it is made by a married person, the spouse must be informed, but his or her consent is not required.

This law would legitimize suicide and thus would clearly break with the Judaeo-Christian ethical tradition as well as with the Hippocratic Oath. But it goes beyond that and in effect would legitimize murder (provided it is done at the victim's request) and thus would create a class of legal killers.

---

[22]Frederick Wertham, *A Sign for Cain* (New York: Macmillan, 1966), p. 190.
[23]1975 Wisconsin legislature, Assembly Bill 1207, the "right to die" bill.

4

How We Got Here

Before I formed you in the womb I knew you.

—Jeremiah 1:5, NASB

The "abortion reform" movement began in earnest in the United States in the early 1960s. Initially, agitation was for the liberalization of criteria for abortion—from the generally accepted life of the mother criterion to include maternal mental and emotional health, rape, incest, and fetal deformity. In 1967, California, Colorado, and North Carolina liberalized their abortion laws in this direction. Ronald Reagan, governor of California at that time, signed the 1967 California bill.

Like many others, he appears never to have suspected the way in which such apparently narrow criteria would be used to create an epidemic of abortions. During the 1976 Republican presidential primaries, Governor Reagan stated that his 1967 decision had been wrong, and he advocated passage of a Human Life Amendment.

In 1970, Hawaii, Alaska, New York, and Washington enacted abortion-on-demand legislation. New York set the most liberal time limit—twenty-four weeks. The situation created in New York hospitals as a result of this law is the basis for Magda Denes's book, *In Necessity and Sorrow.* The New York state legislature repealed the pro-abortion bill the following year, but the repeal was vetoed by Governor Nelson Rockefeller. Rockefeller himself, together with his brother John D. Rockefeller, III, is an outspoken advocate of abortion on demand and other forms of drastic population control.

DEATH BEFORE BIRTH

The impact of the easy abortion laws in New York and elsewhere was becoming common knowledge in the early 1970s. As a result, sentiment nationwide began to turn against abortion on demand. The reversal of position by the New York legislature is a case in point. In November of 1972, there were easy abortion laws on the ballot in Michigan and North Dakota. The eyes of the nation were fixed on those two states to see the public response to liberalized abortion. Contrary to the hopes and expectations of the pro-abortionists, the proposals were overwhelmingly defeated—by a two-to-one margin in Michigan and by a three-to-one margin in North Dakota.

Only two months later, in January of 1973, the U.S. Supreme Court, in two 7–2 decisions, turned the whole nation around and established abortion as a "constitutional right." The major decision, *Roe* v. *Wade,* was so sweeping that it astonished even the most ardent pro-abortionists. No one had expected the right to destroy a developing child right up to the time of birth, an action which is legal in no other civilized society. Judging by Chief Justice Warren D. Burger's concurring opinion, some of the members of the Court apparently had no idea what they were doing. But deliberately or not, the U.S. Supreme Court with *Roe* v. *Wade* made abortion on demand a way of life (or death) for millions of Americans.

As a result of *Roe* v. *Wade,* it is virtually impossible for any state to do anything to protect developing life. This holds true even during the last days prior to birth, although most Americans are unaware of that fact. *Roe* v. *Wade* apparently would allow protection during the final days of pregnancy, but because such protection is explicitly conditioned on "health," as defined in *Doe* v. *Bolton,* it remains for all practical purposes nonexistent. This places the United States alone among all the civilized nations of the world in permitting abortions at such a late point in pregnancy that the fetus, if born prematurely or by normal Caesarean section at that time, would live. Such late abortions are considered in most nations of the world to be infanticide.

Roe v. *Wade* made abortion legal throughout America. It did

74

not, in and of itself, require public financing of abortions any more than public financing of other medical expenses is a constitutional right. (Both federal and state governments fund many personal medical expenses, but they do so on the basis of specific statutes, not as a matter of constitutional right.) However, no sooner had abortion become legal than it also became widely tax-supported. It is estimated that in 1976 approximately one-third of all abortions were funded by federal money, in addition to a large number funded by states. The two major arguments in favor of government funding were based on (1) the view that not to fund for the poor what the rich could legally buy—abortion on demand—constitutes discrimination, and (2) the fact that it is less expensive for the government to finance an abortion than to finance prenatal care, delivery costs, and postnatal care, perhaps involving aid to dependent children and other welfare costs.

The fact that a large proportion of abortion-related costs is being paid by the taxpayer reflects the fact that a large proportion of medical expense in general is now publicly financed. The frustrating thing has been that so much government money has been spent on abortion not merely without specific congressional authorization but in violation of explicit congressional prohibitions.

In October, 1976, Congress passed the HEW appropriations bill with the so-called Hyde Amendment attached, banning the use of federal funds for abortions except where necessary to save the life of the monther. This Hyde Amendment was the result of long and heated deliberation in Congress, and was enacted only in the course of overriding a veto by President Ford (who approved of Hyde but disapproved of the whole HEW budget). Immediately after its passage, federal judge John Dooling in New York granted an injunction against enforcing it, saying it was too vague—in other words, ordering HEW to go on paying, despite the Hyde Amendment. This raised a very serious constitutional question, for only Congress is authorized to spend federal money, and thanks to "Dooling's ruling" HEW was being obliged to spend approximately fifty million dollars for a third of a million abortions—not only without authorization by Congress but *against* its express orders.

The Supreme Court refused to hear appeals directly related to the Hyde Amendment, but in a series of decisions handed down June 22, 1977, determined that individual states are not obliged to pay for elective abortions. In *McRae* v. *Califano*, the Supreme Court then vacated Judge Dooling's order and required him to rehear the case. Dooling quickly issued another temporary order, keeping the HEW abortion money flowing. However, on August 4, 1977, he withdrew his order, and the same day HEW Secretary Joseph A. Califano directed HEW to cease paying for abortions. Thus—as long as the fiscal 1977 HEW budget runs, (until September 30, 1977)—HEW will, it seems, no longer be paying. This does nothing to limit the availability of abortion nor to protect the developing child, but it frees taxpayers at least temporarily from the burden of paying for them through their federal taxes. (Abortions may, and in many places do, continue to be funded through state tax money.)

In the meantime a new HEW appropriations bill is pending (sponsored by Senator Edward Brooke of Massachusetts) which might permit federal funding for such abortions as are called "medically necessary." According to former Assistant HEW Secretary and ardent pro-abortionist population expert Dr. Louis Hellman, as well as pro-life gynecologist Dennis Cavanagh, the bill's language would permit the federal government to resume funding of ninety percent of the abortions it had been funding prior to Califano's decision of August 4, 1977.

What all this means is that with *Roe* v. *Wade* as the "law of the land," not merely is it impossible to protect the unborn child, it is very hard to avoid the obligation to subsidize its destruction. Efforts such as those of Congressman Henry Hyde are commendable, but even when successful offer only slight impediments to the progress of what journalist Nick Thimmesch called "the abortion culture." The tremendous value of the Hyde

Amendment and of the Supreme Court action that appears to recognize Hyde's goals as constitutionally proper is that it has brought the abortion issue squarely into the center of the public arena. If these very modest gains, however, should serve to tranquilize Americans about the whole abortion-euthanasia issue, their long-range effect might be terrible. Several Supreme Court justices who voted against obligatory funding have made it quite clear that they continue to support abortion on demand as the law of the land; they merely do not claim that the federal government has a constitutional obligation to pay for it. There is nothing in these recent decisions to *prevent* any state, or even Congress, from appropriating money to subsidize abortions; they only state that the federal and state governments are *under no obligation* to spend money that has not been appropriated.

All of this is extremely complex and will not be satisfactorily resolved until America—led, we hope, by its Christian citizens—resolves to *protect* innocent life. The fact that the pro-life forces, in August of 1977, were able to achieve at least a tactical victory against the media blitz as well as legal maneuvering of the pro-abortionists indicates that our tenacity and skill are increasing. But it should not distract us from where, as a nation, we still stand as a result of *Roe* v. *Wade*.

What It Says

The *Roe* v. *Wade* decision is relatively short—sixty-four pages. It is also quite clear. It has been analyzed by legal scholars in America and overseas, and while there is tremendous criticism of its wisdom, there is no doubt about its meaning. Nevertheless, it is widely misrepresented. The *Washington Post,* one of America's most influential newspapers, has consistently referred to *Roe* v. *Wade* as permitting *early* abortions,[1] when in fact it permits them at any time during pregnancy, subject to some theoretical

---

[1]E.g., the *Washington Post,* January 23, 1973. As recently as September 27, 1977, *Post* editorial page editor Philip Geyelin declined to correct this misinformation (letter to the author).

restrictions in the last trimester. During the fall of 1976, a Harris poll asked people whether they approved of the U.S. Supreme Court's decision "permitting abortions early in pregnancy." Although this confusion is widespread and sometimes appears to be deliberate, the facts are plain. Let us look in some detail at what *Roe* v. *Wade* says.[2]

Roe v. *Wade* divides the nine months of pregnancy into three trimesters (three-month periods). There is no biological reason for this division; nothing happens to the developing fetus at the end of the third or sixth month that would make it logical to give it different rights. There is a practical medical reason for the division: during the first three months, abortion is possible by a relatively simple operation; during the second three months, a more complex procedure is necessary; and during the last three months, abortion is performed as a hysterotomy, a procedure that delivers a live but immature baby as by a Caesarean section—with the difference that the baby is allowed to die or is killed outright rather than protected and cared for. These are well-known medical facts that require no documentation; they can be confirmed by anyone familiar with abortion techniques and practices.[3]

First Trimester: Abortion on Demand

During the first trimester, according to *Roe* v. *Wade*, the state may make *no* regulations regarding abortion. *Planned Parenthood* v. *Danforth,* July 1, 1976, prohibits the state from requiring the consent of the prospective father or of the parents of a pregnant minor. The freedom to abort is the closest thing to an

---

[2]Supreme Court of the United States, Syllabus, *Roe et al.* v. *Wade,* 1973. This syllabus is published without page numbering; references are to section headings.

[3]Sometimes the first trimester techniques (dilatation and curettage, and suction curettage) are performed early in the fourth month, and sometimes the second-trimester techniques ("salting out," and prostaglandin-induced premature labor) are performed in the third trimester, but the general practice is as outlined here.

absolute freedom possible, it seems. The absence of regulation, of course, allows abortion on demand during the first trimester.

Second Trimester: Abortion on Demand

During the second trimester, according to the Supreme Court, "the State, in promoting its interest in the health of the mother, may, if it chooses, regulate the abortion procedure in ways that are reasonably related to maternal health." In other words, there may be no regulation with respect to the life of the fetus. This too is abortion on demand. The state of Missouri attempted to prohibit the saline technique of second-trimester abortions—something even pro-abortion physicians acknowledge to be relatively more dangerous to maternal health.[4] But the Supreme Court declared this unconstitutional in *Planned Parenthood* v. *Danforth*. Thus, in the second trimester there is no protection for the developing child and absolute freedom to abort it.

Third Trimester: Virtual Abortion on Demand

It is frequently alleged that the Supreme Court at least permits the protection of developing life after "viability." Indeed, the language of *Roe* v. *Wade* seems to say this, but as a matter of actual fact, it doesn't.

What does *Roe* v. *Wade* say? "For the stage subsequent to viability,[5] the State in promoting its interest in the potentiality of

---

[4]See Willard Cates, Jr., M.D., M.P.H. et al., "Legal Abortion Mortality in the United States," *Journal of the American Medical Association* (JAMA), Vol. 237:5 (January 31, 1977), pp. 452–55.

[5]"Viability" is defined by *Roe* v. *Wade* as the ability to survive outside the mother's womb. The Court estimated it at six or seven months. In fact, however, the age at which survival outside the womb is possible is constantly being lowered. The survival of five-month-old fetuses, while not at all common, is not unknown. It is in connection with the criterion of viability that Dr. Denes observes that it is no more reasonable to destroy a child by abortion because it could not live if suddenly delivered than to drown a nonswimmer in a bathtub because he could not live if thrown into the middle of the ocean.

human life[6] may, if it chooses, regulate, and even proscribe [forbid] abortion except where it is necessary, in appropriate medical judgment, for the preservation of the life or health of the mother."

But this apparent concession to the right of the individual state to protect developing life in the final weeks before birth is effectively wiped out by the provision of the same day's decision, *Doe* v. *Bolton,* that health must be taken in its broadest medical context, and must include psychological, emotional, and familial, as well as other factors. Since there is *no* pregnancy that does not have some consequences for a woman's emotional and family situation, this provision has the effect of legalizing abortion right up to the point of birth for any woman who can persuade a doctor that she needs it for reasons of "emotional health." And this is abortion on demand, even in the third and final trimester.

In practice, *Roe* v. *Wade* has been interpreted this way: Late abortions are not performed everywhere, but they are performed in great numbers and no state has successfully forbidden them. Where they are not performed, it is due to restraint on the part of the medical profession or the hospitals, not to prohibition by law.

That is *what* the Court says. But *why* did the Court say it? In order to answer this question satisfactorily, we must look at (1) what the Court gave as its reasons, and (2) the underlying considerations that are not actually stated in *Roe* v. *Wade.* The Court's explicit reasoning in *Roe* v. *Wade* is so strange that it almost forces us to look for hidden motives.

The Court's Reasons

The Court's reasoning is relatively complex. Let us try to state its argument in a logical way, if not necessarily in the order in which the reasons are given in *Roe* v. *Wade.*

---

[6]"Potentiality of human life" is biologically false. Nearly all biologists agree that the fetus is not a "potentiality of life," but rather human life in the process of development.

HOW WE GOT HERE

1. *It is impossible to say when human life begins. The Court may not and need not try to decide this issue.* This is false. Physicians, biologists, and geneticists know that an individual human life begins at conception, with the possible exception of identical twins, where the division of the zygote into two individuals takes place shortly after conception. Biologists agree that a human life *has* begun by nidation or implantation, usually about seven days after conception. The Bible also indicates a new life has begun at conception—e.g., Psalm 51:5: "Behold, I was shapen in iniquity; and in sin did my mother conceive me." However, having decided that it does not know when human life begins, the Court then rather illogically proceeded to grant the total liberty to destroy the fetus, which by its own standards certainly *could* be human life.

2. *Abortion laws are of relatively recent origin;* 3. *Therefore, they are unnecessary.* This is not altogether true, but it is a somewhat complex question. Prohibition of slavery also dates only from the nineteenth century. Should we therefore reintroduce slavery?

4. *Opposition to abortion comes mainly from two sources—the Oath of Hippocrates and Christianity. When the Oath was introduced, it did not correspond to the general view of the ancient world: "Ancient religion did not bar abortion." When prohibition of abortion was widely accepted, this was due to the influence of Christianity. Hence neither the Oath nor Christianity need be considered.* The Court relied heavily on the opening pages of Ludwig Edelstein's *The Hippocratic Oath,* but paid no attention to Edelstein's conclusion. Edelstein argued that the Hippocratic Oath finds natural acceptance as the universal standard of medical ethics "in all countries, in all epochs in which monotheism in its purely religious or its more secular form was the accepted creed."[7]

---

[7]Ludwig Edelstein, *The Hippocratic Oath,* in *Supplements to the Bulletin of the History of Medicine,* No. 1, ed. Henry E. Sigerist (Baltimore: Johns Hopkins, 1943), p. 64.

See also my article, "What the Supreme Court Didn't Know," *Human Life Review,* Vol 1:2 (Spring, 1975), esp. pp. 13–14.

5. *Since the fetus is not a person, and since neither the Hippocratic Oath nor Judaeo-Christian ethics have any weight, the only thing to be considered is the explicit standard set by the Constitution.*

6. *Admittedly abortion is not discussed in the Constitution, but the woman's "right to privacy" is. Actually, the Court was not sure exactly where the "right to privacy" is to be found in the Constitution, but it is sure that it is there (Section VIII).* Even if the right to privacy *were* in the Constitution, one might reasonably ask whether such a personal right (which only needs be temporarily held in check, not destroyed), automatically outweighs the right to life. The right to life also is not mentioned in the Constitution, although it does figure in the Declaration of Independence where we read that it is an endowment of the Creator.

7. *Opposition to the woman's right to privacy is possible only if there is a "compelling state interest" at stake.* Note that in this decision the right to live becomes dependent upon *the interest of the state.*

8. *A "compelling state interest" exists not only when the health of the mother is at stake, but also when there is "capability of meaningful life," which occurs at viability.* The clear implication of this argument is that where life is not meaningful—by whose standard?—the state has no interest, and hence no right to protect it.

9. *Since there is no "compelling state interest" in protecting developing life, the state may not do it.*

10. In subsequent decisions, the Supreme Court also determined that *what the state does not have* (the right to bar an abortion) *it may not grant to anyone else*—specifically, to the father. The direct consequence of this is that a father has no right to protect the life of his own developing child in the grotesque situation in which the prospective mother wants to destroy it. It also implies that no such thing as *natural rights,* created by paternity, exist. *The only human rights are those granted by the state.* As suggested in a California Supreme Court decision, *Serrano* v. *Priest,* the child is "an asset of the state." If the state does not value its "asset," then no one else may protect it either.

HOW WE GOT HERE

The glaring and immediate consequences of the Supreme Court's decision are evident: 1 million abortions (at least) per year; a decline in the birth rate below population replacement levels, with a probable further decline still to come; the virtual disappearance of healthy infants available for adoption; the creation of a large and growing number of women with potential physical and psychological damage from abortion; and the creation of a large and growing segment of the medical profession that makes its living by "terminating" life rather than by protecting it. To understand the long-range consequences, we must look more closely at the Court's reasoning and the mentality that underlies it.

The Court's Ten Steps

If we are going to understand what the future holds, we are going to have to understand the presuppositions and implications of *Roe* v. *Wade*. Let us look more closely at each of the ten reasons given earlier.

1. *The Impossibility of Saying When Human Life Begins.*
The Court's words on this subject sound very modest: "We need not resolve the difficult question of when life begins. When those trained in the respective disciplines of medicine, philosophy, and theology are unable to arrive at any consensus the judiciary, at this point in the development of man's knowledge, is not in a position to speculate as to the answer." [But apparently it *is* in a position to deny that the unborn child is a human being and thus to legalize his destruction, as Justice White complains, "for any . . . reason, or for no reason at all."]
Substantial differences about when human life begins are confined to the ancient Stoic philosophers and to medieval theologians. (The Pythagorean school of philosophy, which originated the Hippocratic Oath, believed with modern science and the Bible that life begins at conception.) Among modern medical and scientific authorities the only disagreement concerns the point at which a distinctive individuality is established,

whether at conception or at nidation (the implantation of the fertilized egg in the wall of the uterus). Nidation occurs approximately seven days after conception; the abortion decision and all the abortion procedures discussed always occur some time *after* nidation. Therefore, the question of whether the individual human life begins at conception or one week later at nidation does not affect the fact that abortion destroys a developing, individual human life.[8]

For the Supreme Court to say there is no consensus as to when life begins is to betray either ignorance or a willingness to deceive. It is as if one were to look at a dog and say, "I cannot tell what kind of an animal it is" because one is uncertain whether it is a Weimaraner or a German Shorthair.

The great majority of pro-abortionists, unlike the Supreme Court, are perfectly aware of what they are doing in an abortion, namely, destroying a developing human life. A pro-abortion editorial, "A New Ethic for Medicine and Society," candidly stated that the only reason for arguing that the fetus is less than human life is that abortion would not be accepted by the public if it were honestly described as what it is. "The very considerable semantic gymnastics which are required to rationalize abortion as anything but the taking of human life would be ludicrous if not often put forth under socially impeccable auspices."[9] How can the "social impeccability" of any authority justify deliberate falsification of the facts? Yet without such falsification, *Roe* v. *Wade* would have been impossible.

It is abundantly evident that the Court is either acting out of a surprising ignorance or it is merely using a pretext to cloak its intention to give complete freedom of abortion. This is particu-

---

[8]This question of whether human life begins at nidation or at conception is relevant to some forms of birth control, namely the intra-uterine device (IUD) and the so-called "morning-after pill," both of which appear to prevent implantation and thus to kill a just-begun human embryo. Where identical twins do not develop, the individual life begins at conception.

[9]"A New Ethic for Medicine and Society," editorial, *California Medicine*, September, 1970, p. 68.

larly obvious when we think of the logical conclusion one would expect reasonable people to draw when confronted with such an open question. If abortion *might* destroy an individual human life, the logical thing to do certainly would be to give the fetus the benefit of the doubt, or at least to seek to protect it wherever possible.

This is why Watergate special prosecutor Archibald Cox faults the Supreme Court for failing even to consider the most important matter at stake—the sanctity of human life: "The opinion fails even to consider what I would suppose to be the most compelling interest of the State in prohibiting abortion: the interest in maintaining that respect for the paramount sanctity of human life which has always been at the centre of Western civilization."[10]

2. Abortion Laws Are of Recent Origin; 3. Therefore, They Are Unnecessary

The Supreme Court makes a great deal of the fact that "the restrictive criminal abortion laws in effect in a majority of States . . . are of relatively recent vintage."[11] This is curious logic. The abolition of slavery is of similarly recent vintage, but no one would propose using that fact as justification for bringing slavery back. The West German Supreme Court found the same situation in German law, but ruled that a right to life that has been recognized for a century or more should not be abrogated. For some strange reason, at the point of abortion, but nowhere else, the Supreme Court wants to go by the most ancient precedents.

The Court's resumé of the historical development begins with ancient Greece and Rome and goes on to the Hippocratic Oath (fourth century B.C.). From the Hippocratic Oath it springs to English common law. The thirteenth-century authority Bracton

[10]Archibald Cox, *The Role of the Supreme Court in American Government* (New York: Oxford, 1976), p. 52.
[11]*Roe* v. *Wade,* VI.

called abortion "homicide," but the Court, relying on two obscure and misinterpreted cases from the fourteenth century supplied by pro-abortion lawyer Cyril Means, concluded it was not a common-law crime.[12] It is remarkable that here, but nowhere else in American law, it is assumed that if the fourteenth century did not know a thing to be wrong, neither should we. "Examination" by torture was a common fourteenth-century practice.

For some reason, the Court skips directly from pre-Christian pagan law to English common law, overlooking eleven centuries of Roman law that contained many explicit prohibitions of abortion. Probably it overlooks later imperial Roman law for the same reason it rejects the Oath of Hippocrates—because it was influenced by Christianity. In any case, it is not true that anti-abortion legislation dates only from the nineteenth century. In America it does; but the U.S. Constitution itself, which created the Supreme Court, is only a few years older than the nineteenth century. If such "recent developments" are without value, then it would make sense to throw out the Supreme Court and return America to the English Crown.

4. *Opposition to Abortion confined to the Pythagoreans and Christians*

The Court did struggle for a moment with the Hippocratic Oath, which has been the standard of medical ethics for almost two and one-half millennia and which does explicitly prohibit abortion. How could our nation's highest court glibly break with almost 2,500 years of ethical tradition? The answer lies in two arguments. First, the Court argued that the Oath did not represent the consensus of the ancient world, but the ideas of a "reform movement," Pythagorean philosophy.

---

[12]Means's study, reportedly written with the aid of a grant from the Playboy Foundation, is a very shabby piece of scholarship for the U.S. Supreme Court to use as a basis for "the law of the land," as shown by Robert A. Destro, "Abortion and the Constitution," *Human Life Review*, Vol. 2:4 (Fall, 1976), esp. pp. 40-44. Cf. *Annual Report,* Playboy Foundation, 1973.

HOW WE GOT HERE

The Pythagoreans believed man is made in the image of God and hence forbade abortion and suicide. Since the Court permits abortion (and will probably soon permit euthanasia), are we to assume that the Court says man is *not* made in the image of God? The Court believes that the Pythagoreans held as a matter of "dogma" the fact that life begins at conception. The Stoics held it to begin at birth. Was Stoic philosophy less "dogmatic" than Pythagorean?

The Court's second argument was that the Hippocratic Oath finally became universal because of the influence of Christianity. The implied conclusion is that therefore the Oath is of no significance. The Court relied heavily on the work of classical scholar Ludwig Edelstein to show that the Oath was not as universal as was thought prior to *Roe* v. *Wade*. But the remarkable thing is that Edelstein, after having shown the Pythagorean origin of the Oath, goes on to acclaim it as the highest expression of medical ethics, hailed wherever people believe in one God. Are we to assume that the Court's researchers were unable to read Professor Edelstein's sixty-odd pages through to the end? Or are we to assume that when they prefer "ancient religion" to the Oath of Hippocrates they are telling us they prefer pagan polytheism to belief in one God?

Of course it is not fair to charge that the Court deliberately attacked Christianity and monotheism in *Roe* v. *Wade*. But it is remarkable that a decision that in effect permits the elimination of 1 million human lives per year would be based on such shabby reasoning and false historical evidence that its inaccuracy can be discovered in one afternoon in a good library.[13]

In some ways this is as depressing as anything that the study of *Roe* v. *Wade* shows, namely, that the justices of our highest court, with all the resources at their command, do such poor work and are willing to reject both traditional Christianity and medical ethics on the basis of incredibly shoddy "research." *Roe* v. *Wade*

[13]I discovered this myself in one day in the Library of Congress. See my article, "What the Court Didn't Know," *Human Life Review*, Vol. 1:2 (Spring, 1975).

bears evidence of being based on a combination of a partial reading of Ludwig Edelstein's short monograph and Cyril Means's two articles on the common-law right to an abortion at any stage of gestation. Perhaps the most charitable thing that can be said about the latter is that the articles are roughly on the level of studies that purport to show that Joan of Arc discovered America.

5. *Only "Constitutional" Arguments Considered*

In writing the majority opinion, Associate Justice Blackmun stated, "Our task, of course, is to resolve the issue by constitutional measurement, free of emotion and of predilection." In a defense of his judicial conduct given at Norfolk, Virginia, in 1976, he reiterated his claim to have acted solely for constitutional reasons. But what has become abundantly clear is that there are in fact no constitutional provisions that cover the abortion question.

Apparently what Justice Blackmun and the six justices who agreed with him believe is that although the Constitution does not by any remotely plausible reasoning touch on the question of abortion, it does set a standard of privacy such that the Court today has to interpret the right to abort as being "constitutional." As Solicitor General Bork wrote in connection with another case, the Court could not reach its decision through principle since the Constitution had not spoken; given that fact, the result depended on the justices' own value preferences.[14]

When we put it in this technical, abstract language, it may sound innocent enough. But the fact is that since 1973, at least 4 million developing human lives have been destroyed in the United States thanks to the value preferences of seven "justices." Each of us who pays taxes in America has contributed to the snuffing out of over 1 million lives, since approximately thirty-five percent of all abortions are tax-funded. Against this

---

[14]Cited by Robert J. Steamer, "Judicial Accountability," *Human Life Review*, Vol 2:4 (Fall, 1976), p. 26.

background, we can understand why George H. Williams, Hollis Professor of Divinity at Harvard University and holder of the nation's most distinguished chair of Protestant theology, calls the present Court an "evil Court." There are no kind words to describe a body that first legitimizes, and then in effect orders, mass liquidations on the basis of its "value preferences."[15]

The "constitutional law" argument in *Roe* v. *Wade* is so bad that the decision was immediately greeted by a chorus of dismay from constitutional lawyers all over the country and legal scholars around the world. Even those who favored abortion realized the Court acted on its own whims, not on the basis of the Constitution.[16] Unfortunately, once the Supreme Court has made a decision on "constitutional" grounds, it cannot be changed short of a constitutional amendment.[17] (Of course, the Supreme Court can reverse itself, but it cannot be influenced to do so by any lawful means.)

[15]Justice Blackmun, author and defender of the *Roe* v. *Wade* decision, has frequently commented on the "hate mail" he has received on the issue. Writing hate-filled letters is neither Christian nor particularly useful. Nevertheless, once one has grasped the full nature of the situation that Blackmun and his six consenting colleagues have created, it is hard to be polite about it. Justice Blackmun's complaints about the grief his "hate mail" causes him sound a bit like Dr. Shaw's comments on the "terrible ordeal" he goes through every time he has to watch a retarded baby die of starvation.

[16]See Prof. John Hart Ely (who *favors* abortion), "The Wages of Crying Wolf," *Human Life Review*, Vol. 1:1 (Winter, 1975), pp. 44–73.

[17]This argument has been well put by Robert J. Steamer, Vice-Chancellor of the University of Massachusetts in Boston, in "Judicial Accountability," *Human Life Review*, Vol. 2:4 (Fall, 1976), pp. 20–29.

In the abortion cases the Supreme Court once again viewed constitutional litigation as a means of settling a major social question and it settled the issue without principle. Justice Blackmun, in speaking for the Court, invoked a constitutional right that is nowhere mentioned in the Constitution, the right to privacy. He had, of course, to rely on other cases, including *Griswold*, in which the Court had also invoked the unarticulated idea that a general right of privacy is guaranteed by the Constitution.

Relying on the due process clause and with the concurrence of six of his brethren, Justice Blackmun rewrote the law of abortion and couched it in constitutional terms, thereby foreclosing all debate on the issue excepting the remote possibility of a constitutional amendment. And he did so without really facing the key question: who is a person? In Justice Blackmun's words,

6. The "Right to Privacy" Includes the "Right to Abort"

Even if the Constitution now contains the "right to privacy" and even if this right includes the right to have an abortion, that does not necessarily settle the issue unless we say that the Constitution is the equal of the Word of God.

Whether or not the Court has logically interpreted the Constitution, the fact remains that *Roe* v. *Wade* and *Planned Parenthood* v. *Danforth* are now "the law of the land." Arthur S. Flemming, chairman of the U.S. Civil Rights Commission, argues in his commission's report that once the Court has discovered a "constitutional right," amending the Constitution would itself be unconstitutional.[18]

The Constitution, according to Supreme Court decisions, used to prohibit a federal income tax. The Sixteenth Amendment was passed and we now have a federal income tax. Flemming's argument is so silly that it seems to be a new fulfillment of what Paul said about ancient pagans: "Professing themselves to be wise, they became fools" (Rom. 1:22). Since the Constitution provides for amendments, how can it be unconstitutional to

the Court "need not resolve the difficult question of when life begins," but need only look at the harm which might devolve upon the mother which might be "psychological" or simply "distressful" as a result of giving birth to additional offspring.

I cannot improve upon Professor Epstein's analysis of why this decision is so constitutionally vacuous [Richard A. Epstein, "Substantive Due Process By Any Other Name," (Chicago: The Supreme Court Review, 1973)]. If the unborn is not a person, says Epstein, it is difficult to see why either the woman who requests an abortion or the doctor who performs it owes anyone an explanation for what they have done. The decision to end a pregnancy is a personal preference which needs no justification because it suggests no wrong. Remove a hangnail, terminate a pregnancy, it is all the same thing.

But if we decide that the unborn child is a person, we must find some justification for deliberately killing a human being. Had the child been born, the mother could not have killed it at birth for the reason that the child would have forced upon the woman, in Blackmun's phrase, "a distressful life and future." This is a brutal justification for deliberate killing, and if the unborn child is a person, the logic of Mr. Justice Blackmun's position collapses (pp. 26–27).

[18]*Constitutional Aspects of the Right to Limit Childbearing,* U.S. Commission on Civil Rights, April, 1975, esp. pp. 27–43.

amend it? The answer is that Flemming *prefers* things the way they now stand, thanks to *Roe* v. *Wade*, and therefore argues that any change is impossible.

What does the Constitution represent? Why does it command our obedience? There are two possible views. First is the view that it represents the embodiment of a higher law, the law of God, for example, or what philosophers call natural law. Certainly this is what the founding fathers thought they were doing in writing the Constitution—not "creating" principles, but recognizing principles of God's law or of natural law. The second view is that the Constitution represents the will of the people. It says whatever the people want it to say.

If the Constitution represents a higher law, then it should be possible to correct it and change it in light of the law. If it represents the will of the people, then it should be possible to change it if the people want it changed. So Chairman Flemming's view that it cannot be changed once the Court has interpreted it makes a mockery of the basic theory of American government. One can be certain that if the Court had discovered in the Constitution a fundamental right to life instead of a right to privacy, Flemming and his friends would be loudly demanding a constitutional amendment to safeguard the right to privacy and the right to abortion.[19]

In a recent series of Supreme Court decisions and federal laws, the "right to privacy" has been almost abolished with respect to financial transactions. Banks must keep and furnish to the government on demand elaborate records of all transactions by their customers, and they are not required to tell their customers when they do it. Federal agents have the right to enter businesses and confiscate their records without respect for the "right to privacy." It seems that this "right" is a very flexible

---

[19]It is a strange commentary on Mr. Flemming's views that he holds that every child has the right to cross-district, compulsory bussing for racial integration, but he doesn't have the right to life. You don't have to let him live, but if you do, you have to bus him.

one, applying to hospitals for the purposes of abortion but not to individuals for banking transactions. Or, to put it bluntly, what you do with your money is more important to the federal government than what you do with human lives.

7.–9. *"Compelling State Interest" and "Meaningful Life"*

Having discovered the "right to privacy," the Court ruled that governments may not interfere with it unless there is a "compelling state interest." (The state does have a "compelling interest" in money, which explains why the "right to privacy" evaporates where financial transactions are concerned!) Apparently what the Court means by "compelling state interest" is that where the subject concerned is not of sufficient value to the state, the state has no interest in it or right to protect it. This is a total reversal of fundamental American values: the rights of individuals do not come from their value to the state, but from the Creator. It doesn't take much imagination to see where the doctrine of "compelling state interest" will lead us when bureaucrats begin to add up the cost of caring for the old, the handicapped, the retired, and even those who are underproducers.

From this perspective, it would have been better if the Court had simply ruled that the unborn child is not a human being until birth. This would have been medically and scientifically false, but it would have spared us the implications of what follows. Then, at least, it would have been logical enough to allow the woman and her physician to destroy it. But the Court specifically stated it is not necessary to determine when life begins. All that is necessary is to see whether the life has a "compelling interest" to the state. And clearly the life of the developing fetus will cost money rather than produce it, especially if the mother doesn't want it.

A human being is of "compelling interest" only when it has the "capability of meaningful life." In *Roe* v. *Wade*, the Court meant something very specific by "capability of meaningful life." It meant the ability to live outside the mother's body. But now it has established that the state's interest depends on the "meaningfulness" of a person's life, which is a very subjective thing. It is also very easy to see that this doctrine can be used to classify quite a few of us as "meaningless" and therefore of no "compelling interest" to the state.

10. *No Rights Except as the State Gives Them*

In *Planned Parenthood* v. *Danforth* the Supreme Court carried the logic of *Roe* v. *Wade* one step further. In *Roe* v. *Wade* the Court ruled that the state may not protect developing life unless it is of compelling interest to the state. *Planned Parenthood* v. *Danforth* ruled that the state may not require the consent of the father of an unborn child or of the parents of an unmarried, pregnant minor for an abortion to be performed. "What the State does not possess, it cannot delegate to another" (the father or the parents). What this says is that *there are no natural rights.* There are only the rights the state is willing to grant.

For six thousand years of recorded history, all societies have recognized the parents' rights and duties to their children. One of the most horrible features of the slave-owning societies of the past was the fact that the slaves had no right to their own children; they too became the property of the slaveowners. Thanks to *Planned Parenthood* v. *Danforth,* the father has in effect been deprived of all rights to his unborn child. If *Roe* v. *Wade* reverted to the moral standards of Roman paganism, *Planned Parenthood* v. *Danforth* falls below them. Even pagan Rome recognized that a father has rights to his natural descendants. But the Supreme Court said that unless those descendants are of "compelling interest" to the state, they may be of interest to no one.

Although Malcolm Muggeridge was writing about the situation in Britain, his words are prophetic: "The abortion issue raises the question of the very destiny and purpose of life itself; of whether our human society is to be seen in Christian terms as a family with a loving father who is God, or as a factory-farm whose primary consideration must be the physical well-being of the livestock and the material well-being of the collectivity."[20]

The Hidden Reasons

Before looking in detail at the specifics of the Court's logic, let's think for a moment about what its subconscious, or at least unexpressed, reasons for *Roe* v. *Wade* may have been. There are two that always come up: the "population explosion" is vaguely mentioned by Justice Blackmun in his preamble to *Roe* v. *Wade*, and women's rights. Although not explicit in *Roe* v. *Wade*, the latter is always presented as an argument in favor of abortion. Both of these unexpressed reasons effectively prejudge what the Court said it could not decide, namely, when human life begins.

If human life has already begun in the mother's womb, then the population explosion is no better an argument for abortion than it is for infanticide or killing people at any other time of their lives. If human life has begun, then no one else's "right to privacy" should give her the right to destroy it. And so it is these hidden or tacit assumptions behind *Roe* v. *Wade* that make it even more dangerous than it may appear: (1) that we do not need to ask the question of whether the fetus is human or when human life begins; (2) that population control is sufficient reason for destroying what by the Court's own logic *may be* human life; and (3) that a woman's desire for privacy or a particular direction of "self-fulfillment" overrides another individual's very right to life.

A great deal has been said about a woman's right to "control her own body." The difficulty arises when the question is faced of whether another person is in that body. And that is precisely what the Court did not answer. Except in the case of forcible rape, the woman has participated in the decision to do some-

---

[20]Malcolm Muggeridge, "What the Abortion Argument Is About," *Human Life Review*, Vol. 1:3 (Summer, 1975), p. 4.

thing that may result in the conception of a human being. Her unlimited right to self-control becomes limited the moment there is another life at stake.

But even so, limiting the woman's right to control her body by saying she cannot destroy a developing human life only temporarily and partially curtails her supposed right. She can deliver the child and then resume the right to total control. The child's right, however, cannot be temporarily limited or suspended. If it is taken, it is gone.

One could reasonably argue that carrying a pregnancy may not be as "distressful" (to borrow Blackmun's term) as taking care of a baby—particularly if it is handicapped or sick. If the woman has the right to exercise control by killing the developing child, why not by destroying a much more bothersome one who has already been born? *As a matter of fact, this is being done.*[21] But most people would not grant the right to infanticide, even of the handicapped and defective. Why not? Because infants, even the handicapped and defective, are human beings and are entitled to the protection of the law. This is the crucial issue in the abortion debate: the humanity of the unborn. It is precisely the issue the Supreme Court bypassed. Will it be bypassed again when we discover just how distressful it is to take care of handicapped, defective, or aged human beings?

Population pressure is certainly a factor in the Supreme Court's decision. Indeed, unchecked population growth is a problem. But as a matter of fact, the American birth rate is already below replacement rate. Far from programming a "population explosion," we are programming a population collapse.

But even if we were facing a population explosion, would that legitimize abortion? Clearly, abortion "controls" population growth. So do epidemics, automobile accidents, murder, war,

[21]Death (usually by starvation) is now widely regarded as the "treatment of choice" for certain conditions, as we have already discussed. See *Death, Dying, and Euthanasia*, Dennis J. Horan and David Mall, eds. (Washington: University Publications, 1977).

concentration camps, and atomic bombs. If we say that we must have abortion because of the population explosion, then we are saying that the end justifies the means. And if the end justifies the means, then why not allow euthanasia? Why not encourage immediate capital punishment of all troublesome offenders? Why not permit forced sterilization, as India has done?

Until the Supreme Court can give us some plausible reasons for its action, we will either have to conclude, with Professor Steamer, that (1) it has acted *without principle,* or (2) we will have to look for hidden reasons, such as a false view of women's rights, the population explosion, and the concept that the end justifies the means.

5

How It Really Works: the "Little Ghosts"

I didn't know it would be like that.

—Comment by one of her judges at the burning of Joan of Arc

Several months ago, a friend picked up a photo lying on our mantlepiece.

"Good heavens! What is this?" she asked.

I told her it was a widely circulated photo of four dead babies in a black plastic disposal bag—the "product" of one morning's "work" at a Canadian abortion facility.

"I didn't know it looked like that," she said in horror.

"Jane," I replied, "you have four children. What did you think it would look like?"

No judge should sentence anyone to a punishment if he himself has no idea what it will be like. And no one dealing with the subject of abortion should neglect to find out what it is really like.

Anti-abortionists have been hotly denounced for "inflammatory, emotional" presentations—pictures of bloody fetuses, severed limbs, salt-burned, swollen little faces, and all the rest of the images that accompany abortion. But there is a place for such things. Maybe the judge who sentenced Joan of Arc to be burned at the stake never again passed such a sentence after watching that burning. Or maybe he became accustomed to it, grew indifferent, or perhaps even got to like it.

The instinctive reaction of most people to the visual side of abortion is one of revulsion and horror. For this reason, pro-abortionists usually do their utmost to ban visual aids from the discussion and even from the classroom. But sometimes the visual aids are almost counterproductive; people get used to the horror. Some doctors find it easier and easier to do later and later abortions.

There aren't going to be any of those pictures in this book. But because one picture *is* worth a thousand words, any reader who has even begun to suspect the seriousness of the abortion situation is encouraged to look at two presentations. One is the award-winning French film *The First Days of Life.* This thirty-minute production has nothing to do with abortion. It shows the development of the human baby from conception to birth and does it in a masterful way. Anyone who sees it will have a deeper insight into the meaning of the psalmist's acclamation, "I am fearfully and wonderfully made: marvelous are thy works; and that my soul knoweth right well" (Ps. 139:14). And no one will walk away from it wondering whether the fetus is human.[1]

A second presentation is that offered by Dr. and Mrs. J. C. Wilke in *Handbook on Abortion.*[2] There you will find the details, the pictures, and the other information you need to form a very graphic idea of what abortion is and what it looks like. Here we will just discuss it without pictures. But even a detailed discussion without a single photograph can be gruesome. We will look first at the techniques, then at the women, the men, and finally at the doctors and hospital or clinic personnel.

The Techniques

As described in the previous chapter, the U.S. Supreme Court

---

[1]*The First Days of Life* is available for a nominal rental fee from your state's Right to Life Committee as well as from other pro-life organizations.
[2]Dr. and Mrs. J. C. Wilke, *Handbook on Abortion* (Cincinnati: Hiltz, 1972).

divided pregnancy into three trimesters. There is no medical or scientific reason for considering the end of the third or the sixth month as marking a distinct change in the nature of the developing fetus. As Dr. Ehrhardt put it, "The embryo is more than a potentiality of life: he *is* human life in the process of development, a development that is completed, in purely bodily terms, only after about twenty years . . . . we can only take note of stages of development within one and the same course of life."[3] However, the techniques of abortion do change after roughly twelve weeks of pregnancy and again after twenty-four (the end of the first and second trimesters, respectively). It almost looks as though *Roe* v. *Wade* was written with the *techniques* of abortion rather than its *morality* in mind. In fact, this is part of Watergate special prosecutor Archibald Cox's accusation against the Supreme Court in *The Role of the Supreme Court in American Government*.[4]

The First Trimester

According to recent government statistics, about eighty-five percent of the abortions in America are done during the first trimester of prenatal life. The techniques of first-trimester abortion were discussed in chapter 3. Since the fetus is still quite small at twelve weeks, weighing hardly more than an ounce, it might seem that scarcely anything is being destroyed in such an early abortion. But the infant's complete heredity (determining its sex; eye, hair, and skin color; height; general weight; facial appearance; and many, many other factors) is present from conception, from the moment the male's sperm unites with the female's ovum. By twelve weeks, the embryo's heart has already been beating for eight weeks; it has had brain activity for six

[3]Helmut E. Ehrhardt, M.D., Ph.D., "Abortion and Euthanasia: Common Problems," *Human Life Review*, Vol. 1:3 (Summer, 1975), pp. 16–17.

[4]Archibald Cox, *The Role of the Supreme Court in American Government* (New York: Oxford, 1976), p. 114.

weeks; it has been moving and is just beginning to suck its thumb.

In hospital interviews, one physician spoke of seeing "a miniature person, so to speak," saying he feels guilty because both the Oath of Hippocrates and the corresponding Jewish Oath of Maimonedes forbid abortion.[5]

Perhaps the best comment on this attitude comes from the decision of the Federal Constitutional Court of West Germany in rejecting the German Bundestag's so-call "time-limit" rule that would permit abortions during the first trimester: "The time-limit rule would lead to a disappearance of the general awareness of the fact that unborn life is worthy of protection during the first three months of pregnancy. It would give credence to the view that abortion, at least in the early period of pregnancy, is just as subject to the free determination of the pregnant woman as is the prevention of pregnancy."[6] The West German court also observed that if abortions up to twelve weeks are seen as permissible, then later abortions will also seem to be permissible. And we have seen from present-day America that where late abortions are permissible, early "postnatal" killing is also being accepted.

The Second Trimester

According to 1974 HEW figures, just under fifteen percent of all American abortions were "late." For some reason HEW does not distinguish between "late" (second trimester) and "very late" (last trimester) abortions in its statistics. Presumably the majority of the late abortions were done in the second trimester. Although third-trimester abortions, usually performed as hysterotomies, are legal, there is still great reluctance on the part of

---

[5]Cited by Magda Denes, *In Necessity and Sorrow*, p. 140.

[6]*Bundesverfassungsgericht* BGB1. I.S. 1297, cited in *Neues Juristisches Wochenblatt*, 1975:13, p. 586, translation by Harold O. J. Brown in *Human Life Review*, Vol. 1:3 (Summer, 1965), p. 84.

many physicians and medical personnel to perform them. However, with a base of 1 million or more abortions per year, the number of very late abortions is still high. A very incomplete report on 73,000 legal abortions was compiled by Dr. Christopher Tietze's Population Council for 1970–1971.[7] The report indicated 1.3 percent hysterotomy abortions. Multiplied by 1 million, that indicates 13,000 hysterotomy abortions per year. Since these figures are largely from New York in the years 1970–71, when hysterotomy abortions there were illegal, it is fair to assume that the actual overall percentage today is higher than 1.3 percent.

In any case, approximately 150,000 abortions per year are "late," the majority of them occurring during the second trimester. Although the Supreme Court vaguely defined "viability" (the time after which an infant might survive outside the womb) as six or seven months, some babies have survived at twenty-two weeks or even less.[8] A fair number of second-trimester abortion babies are delivered alive, but are so badly injured by the abortion procedure that they die shortly afterward. What is the second-trimester procedure?

Basically, the way a child is aborted during the second trimester is by provoking a miscarriage. Accidentally caused premature deliveries and miscarriages have been known since ancient times; the Bible and the ancient Babylonian Code of Hammurabi make reference to them. (See Exodus 21:22–25.) The "father of gynecology," Soranus of Ephesus (late first or early second century A.D.), described cases in which women attempted to provoke a miscarriage by violent exercise. But such

---

[7]The basis for the report, *Legalized Abortion and the Public Health* (Report of the National Academy of Sciences' Institute of Medicine, May, 1975), was the JPSA (Joint Program for the Study of Abortion) Study undertaken by the Population Council, a militantly pro-abortion agency. The study covered 73,000 legal abortions in 1970–71, *when third trimester abortions were still illegal in New York State,* the abortion Mecca of that period.

[8]One of my former students at Trinity Evangelical Divinity School has a daughter who was born prematurely at six months' gestation.

techniques were unreliable and dangerous. Modern medical science has found ways that are guaranteed to provoke a miscarriage with relatively little danger to the woman involved. The most common technique is the saline abortion, sometimes called "salting out."

In a saline abortion the woman is given a local anesthesia. The physician then punctures the lining of the uterus with a needle, withdraws a certain amount of the amniotic fluid surrounding the baby, and replaces it with a strong saline solution. After witnessing his first saline abortion, a physician wrote:

> I close my eyes. I see the inside of the uterus. . . . I see the creature curled upon itself. . . .
>
> It resembles . . . a sleeping infant.
>
> Its place is entered by something. . . . A needle!
>
> The needle comes closer in the pool. The point grazes the thigh, and I stir. . . . My hand finds the shaft—grabs! I *grab*. I bend the needle this way and that. . . . All is a commotion and a churning. There is a presence in the pool. An activity! The pool colors, reddens, darkens. . . .
>
> I know. We cannot feed the great numbers. . . . It is woman's right to refuse the risk, to decline the pain of childbirth. . . .
>
> And yet . . . there is the flick of that needle. I *saw* it. . . . I *felt*—in that room, a pace away, life prodded, life fending off. I saw life avulsed—swept by flood, blackening—then *out*. [9]

The doctor went on, indicating that a physician obviously knows what is going on; he can admit it to himself or repress it. Whether or not to admit it to the patient is a different matter. Within several hours after the fetus has been killed, labor will begin, and shortly the woman will deliver a dead fetus.

Because of the salt, saline abortion babies are discolored and blistered. They are sometimes jestingly called "cherry-apple babies." Seldom does the woman who has had an abortion see the aborted baby; when she does, her impression may be one of horror, as was Dr. Denes's on inspecting saline abortion fetuses. Occasionally a saline abortion baby will be delivered before it is

[9]Richard Selzer, "What I Saw at the Abortion," *Esquire,* Vol. 85:1 (January, 1976), p. 67.

dead, although in such cases it usually is too badly damaged to survive. A few such babies have survived and been adopted.

The saline abortion technique, although "relatively" safe, does present some danger for the woman. The needle may miss the uterus or it may penetrate a blood vessel, causing internal bleeding or perhaps salt poisoning of the woman's bloodstream. When it reaches the fetus, the child wriggles and squirms, often upsetting the abortionist. For this reason, more abortionists are turning to injections of prostaglandins (muscle-affecting substances) instead of salt. The prostaglandins cause the woman to go into labor and deliver a premature fetus. Because there has been no poisoning, prostaglandin abortion fetuses are still alive when delivered. However, because of their immaturity almost all die soon after being delivered.

To avoid the psychological turmoil caused among delivery room personnel by the arrival of doomed premature babies, two techniques are available. A poison can be introduced with the prostaglandins and the baby is delivered dead, or a blue dye can be added, resulting in the delivery of an artificially blue baby. Since hospital personnel know premature blue babies cannot live, they feel less trauma over them.

One of the provisions of Missouri's new abortion law was the prohibition of saline abortions. Although a case can be made for the danger to the woman in this procedure, the U.S. Supreme Court, in *Planned Parenthood* v. *Danforth,* ruled this provision of the Missouri law invalid on the grounds that the saline technique is the most common means of second-trimester abortions. (Shooting is also the most common form of homicide.)[10]

The Hysterotomy

The most astonishing of all abortion practices is the so-called hysterotomy abortion (from Greek *hysteris,* "womb," and *tomein,* "to cut"). A hysterotomy (opening of the uterus) is to be distin-

---

[10]Read Dr. Denes's own reaction to her inspection of a roomful of buckets containing the "remains" of a day's work at the abortion hospital (*In Necessity and Sorrow,* pp. 60-61).

guished from a hysterectomy (removal of the uterus). In a hysterotomy, an incision is made in the lower abdomen which exposes the uterus; the uterus is cut open and the fetus is removed. The procedure up to this point is exactly the same as in a Caesarean section, but now the great difference begins to appear.

The purpose of a Caesarean section is to save a baby—and perhaps the mother too—when the baby cannot safely be delivered normally. The purpose of a hysterotomy is to kill the baby lest it be delivered normally. A hysterotomy always delivers a living fetus. If it is six or seven months premature, then under normal circumstances it cannot long survive, and all the attending physician has to do is to lay it aside on a cold table while he turns his attention back to the "mother." Older and larger fetuses have a greater chance of survival. Therefore something must be done.

If some of the fetuses delivered by hysterotomy were not "dealt with," they would survive. And then the woman would have just what the hysterotomy was intended to prevent—a living, perhaps slightly damaged infant—plus all the trouble of a hysterotomy. Therefore many physicians, if they will do late abortions at all, take a few simple precautions. While the baby is still in the womb, before it is brought out into the air, the umbilical cord, which supplies the baby's oxygen, is clamped or pinched off. Then within a few minutes the baby suffocates and it can "safely and legally" be brought into the open.

The trial of Boston abortionist Dr. Kenneth Edelin involved just such a situation. He delivered a baby boy by Caesarean section after the baby had survived two attempts at a saline abortion. Dr. Edelin took the precaution of clamping the artery before removing the baby from the mother's womb. A Massachusetts jury found him guilty of manslaughter for failing to care for the delivered child, who appeared to be alive on delivery despite all Edelin's precautions. His defense argued that the child could not have survived because the damage (caused by Dr. Edelin, let us note) was already irreversible.

Edelin was named "physician of the year" by Boston University School of Medicine's 1976 graduating class. He was given a hero's welcome in Atlanta by the city's mayor, Maynard Jackson. Ultimately his conviction was overturned on appeal. The *Chicago Tribune* commented editorially that it would be senseless to make a physician liable for doing something, namely killing, a few moments after delivery that would have been perfectly legal minutes earlier while the baby was still out of sight within its mother's womb.

The Edelin case involves a number of macabre aspects. The *Tribune's* logic, in general followed by the Massachusetts Superior Court and by Pennsylvania courts in a similar acquittal in the 1974 case of Dr. Leonard Laufe, is that it is not wrong to neglect to care for a dying individual if the reason for his dying is that you have previously partially strangled him. If such logic were to be accepted, the Nuremburg trials should have acquitted all those physicians who could claim they had experimented only on prisoners who were already slated to die.

Even more sinister is the acclaim Dr. Edelin received for his "courageous" conduct. Only a few years ago, abortion was universally considered a shameful act. Even if Dr. Edelin were totally free of all subjective and objective guilt in successfully terminating the life of that little premature boy, it is hard to see that he did something worthy of popular admiration.

Summary

To the medical layman, the abortion of an eight-month-old fetus, like those in the Laufe and Edelin cases, clearly seems a case of infanticide. Juries, like most operating room personnel, are horrified at the spectacle. The same laymen find it hard to see as much harm in the abortion of a fetus a few weeks old, one that weighs only an ounce or two. But doctors know that in principle there is no difference between early and late abortions. The fetus is just as much a human being at ten weeks as it will be at twenty, thirty, or forty weeks—or at ten, twenty, thirty, or forty years. Many doctors, quite logically, reason that if society legitimizes the destruction of early fetuses, then they cannot reasonably be expected to have scruples about destroying late ones.

The report of the Institute of Medicine tells us, and HEW abortion surveillance head Willard Cates, Jr., M.D., affirms, that legal abortion in the first trimester is "almost nine times safer" than childbirth.[11] It is hard to avoid the impression that such writers *prefer* abortion to childbirth. This is one of the macabre aspects of the American abortion controversy. German and French authorities, for example, even while arguing for the legalization of abortion, never cease to treat it as deplorable and tragic. American doctors such as Tietze, Cates, and Robbins write of it in a value-free way. A perceptive comment on what this means for the medical profession comes from Helmut Ehrhardt, professor of legal and social psychiatry at the University of Marburg, Germany:

> If we assume for the moment that the possibility of a defensible "selection" of cases of "worthless life" has been achieved and legally regulated, then we face the merciless question as to who is to act as the "killing agent" here. Many physicians, including those who feel no special religious commitment, categorically reject such killing. . . . In the case of doctors who indicate that they would be ready to take part, there arises in all seriousness the question of their professional ethics and their character.[12]

America does have its doctors who are willing to act as the "killing agent." And what do we think of them? We make them heroes, "men of the year," and give them the keys to our cities.

The Women

It is impossible to write against abortion without in some sense criticizing the women who get abortions. The pagan Roman

---

[11]Willard Cates, Jr. et al., "Legal Abortion Mortality in the United States," *Journal of the American Medical Association* (JAMA), Vol. 237:5 (January 31, 1977), p. 452.

[12]Ehrhardt, "Abortion and Euthanasia, pp. 29–30.

poet Ovid stated, "The first one who thought of detaching from her womb the fetus forming in it deserved to die by her own weapons." Indeed, that is what happened often enough when abortion was attempted in antiquity. For this reason the great fourth-century Christian Basil of Caesarea called the woman who had an abortion a double murderess: "Accountability is demanded not only for the child that should have been born, but also for the woman, who endangered herself."[13] As both the pagan Ovid and the Christian Basil recognized, abortion in those days involved great risk to the woman. And surely no woman would have risked it unless she was in terrible distress, perhaps even despair. Today we have reduced the risk to the woman's life and so it stands to reason that women will ask for abortions for less desperate problems.

Even so, we must recognize that no woman gladly seeks an abortion. No matter what she tells herself, no matter what sympathetic "abortion counseling" is given to her by pro-abortion clergy, no matter how much the women's libbers insist on her "right to her own body," there is hardly a woman who fails to be deeply affected by her abortion.

Magda Denes, who claims that all abortions are "heart-rending, ambivalent events of absolute necessity" apparently cannot quite believe it. Her book is written in reaction to her own experience with abortion; she entered the hospital three times for the abortion of what would have been her third child. The first two times she called it off; the third time she expected her husband to intervene, but he didn't. Her book is dedicated to her two sons, Greg and Tim, "whose small faces," she says, "are the most moving arguments I have against going through with this abortion." But she did. And she had to write about it.

Not every woman who has gone through an abortion has as much hesitance or as many qualms as Dr. Denes. Yet it is hard to find a woman who has had an abortion without being affected by it. Another testimony, this one by an anonymous Jane Doe,

[13]Basil of Caesarea, *Letters,* 118, 2.

was published on the Op-Ed page of *The New York Times*. It concludes:

> It certainly does make more sense not to be having a baby right now—we say that to each other all the time. But I have this ghost now. A very little ghost that only appears when I'm seeing something beautiful, like the full moon on the ocean last weekend. And the baby waves at me. And I wave at the baby. "Of course, we have room," I cry to the ghost. "Of course, we do."[14]

Not many women are as analytical as Magda Denes or as eloquent as "Jane Doe." But with more than 1 million abortions in America every year, there must be many, many little ghosts in the minds of American women.

So far there are no adequate studies available of the psychological impact of abortion on women; the medical and physiological impact, although virtually denied by the National Academy of Science's report, is well documented (see chapter 3). It seems fair to conclude that by HEW's promotion of an abortion mentality, America is building up a tremendous mass of psychological and emotional disturbance, one that will probably unload itself in hatred for life and perhaps in increasing hatred on the part of women for men in general.

The Men

What happens to the men whose developing children are aborted? If we do not yet know enough about the woman's reaction to an abortion, even less is known about the man's. Generally speaking, "unwanted pregnancy" (especially in the case of the unmarried) is taken to be the woman's problem. It is she who consults the doctor, makes the arrangements, goes through the procedure, and bears the scars. It is she who will

---

[14]*The New York Times*, May 14, 1976. Curiously, "Jane Doe" has reportedly been at pains to present herself, like Dr. Denes, as "pro-abortion." It is hard to distinguish this position from support of what George F. Will calls "discretionary killing."

have the guilt feelings, who will see the "little ghost" if there is one.

Sometimes the man, particularly if he is the woman's husband, will participate in the abortion decision, go with her to see the gynecologist and abortion counselors, and even accompany her to the hospital. But there is one place he cannot go: into the "abortion chamber." There is a growing movement to have fathers present in the delivery room for the birth of a child; as far as I know, there is no movement to have the involved man present at the abortion of an unwanted child. I have never heard of a man wanting to be there.

Since the beginning of time, mankind has lived in families and the "normal" place for conception and birth has been within marriage. One of the major purposes of marriage as a social institution is to "domesticate" men, to teach them responsibility for the children they beget. Without marriage, as George Gilder argues in *Sexual Suicide*,[15] the natural tendency would be for men to roam around in hunting bands, visiting the women from time to time for sexual pleasure, but leaving them with all the responsibility for the children.

Whether or not Gilder's sociology is accurate, it is true that social stability requires familial stability. This means the men must share in caring for, providing for, and educating the children they beget. With responsibilities come rights. In ancient Roman society, the *paterfamilias* (head of the family) had far-reaching rights over the lives of his children. He could order defective or otherwise unwanted children "exposed" (abandoned in a desolate place to starve or be eaten by wild animals). He could even put an older child to death for an infamous or shameful deed.

With the introduction of Christianity, these practices were repudiated and abandoned. The father could no longer kill his offspring. But he did have a great deal to say about their educa-

[15]George Gilder, *Sexual Suicide* (New York: Quadrangle, 1973), esp. pp. 12–43.

tion and work, along with his responsibility to provide for them. In the case of a child born out of wedlock, traditional societies have had ways of making the father fulfil his responsibility; the "shotgun wedding" is only one example. Swedish law holds that a father has the same duties to his child whether it is born in or out of wedlock.

But what happens to the father's responsibilities and rights when abortion on demand becomes the law of the land? His rights evaporate. *Planned Parenthood* v. *Danforth* denies him the right to prevent the abortion of his developing child, even though, one of the dissenting justices pointed out, it might be the only descendant he would ever have. And with his rights gone, his responsibilities will be quick to follow. Why should a man be responsible for a child when the woman had the sole right to determine whether or not it should be born? It will probably be impossible to continue the old practice of holding the fathers of out-of-wedlock children responsible for a share of their care and education.

But fathers are still affected by abortions. The child that is destroyed because it is "unwanted" is, genetically speaking, fifty percent the father's. If he has participated in the abortion decision, he too knows he has destroyed a part of his posterity, a part of his link to the future. He has committed a crime against his own family and blood, not altogether different from consenting to the death of a child who has been born. We can imagine that the natural reaction of a father to a doctor or anyone else who attempted to kill his living child would almost certainly be violent. Is this situation so radically different from that in which a doctor, at the "mother's" request, destroys a developing child? And in the second case, the not-quite father, instead of protecting the child as would be natural, must thank and pay the doctor.

Clearly, the role of the male parent in an abortion is less intense than that of the woman. But it cannot altogether be overlooked. Men as well as women know the facts of life. If we think of 1 million abortions in America per year, we may well think about the possible guilt of 1 million men being added to that of those women who thirty years from now, if not today, will have "little ghosts." How many men will wonder what might have become of the children they destroyed?

From "Protector" To Exploiter"

Dr. Denes points to the acute embarrassment men seem to feel in the abortion situation. Our culture has impressed upon men the conviction that they are to protect their women and, if necessary, to suffer in their place. Women's liberation and the equal rights movement have changed some of our practices and beliefs on this subject, but it is difficult for a society to forget six thousand years of well-established tradition.

No man feels right about letting a woman undergo suffering because he is unwilling to take responsibility for a child or to help her bear it. The man knows the woman would not have had this "problem" apart from him. But there is no way, short of the traditional way of helping her rear the child, that he can get her out of it without some suffering on her part. Even if he pays the bill, she is the one who faces the knife, or the needle, or the curette. Fathers traditionally celebrate the birth of a child; it is hard to celebrate its abortion.

What will this mean for men? If it becomes a common practice for the man's responsibility in sex, and sometimes even in marriage, to end at the abortionist's door, this will certainly have a big impact on the relationships between men and women. If women feel exploited in the traditional family situation, what will they feel like when abortion is the universal answer to a man's responsibility? And what will men have for a self-image when they are forced to realize that their attitude to the opposite sex is no longer one of protection but of exploitation?

Today's society is experiencing drastic changes in the self-image and sex-role identification of men and women. Some of these changes may be desirable and beneficial. But it is hard to see how either sex can benefit from a situation in which the males can revert back to the "hunting bands" of Gilder's imagery, no longer leaving their women with the babies, but leaving them at the abortionist's door. One million exploited women, 1 million male exploiters, and 1 million tiny, innocent victims are added to the rolls each year. What can this mean for the society of the future?

Most pro-abortionists, except for those commercially involved, of course, speak of their desire to reduce the number of abortions. Responsible pro-abortionists for the most part are aware of the difficulties and problems to which I have referred. It is hard to imagine any socially responsible person feeling that abortion is preferable to the alternatives—contraception or birth. Thus in the material Planned Parenthood distributes (largely at federal expense), for high-school sex education, abortion is discouraged. In the Planned Parenthood Federation of America's 1973 publication, *Sex Alphabet,* we read:

TERMINATION OF PREGNANCY

Also known as induced abortion, this is a way of ending pregnancy but before birth. Induced abortion should *not* be considered a preferred method of birth control but a procedure to be used when contraceptives have failed or for personal or medical reasons.[16]

Very few pro-abortionists fail to give lip service to the goal of reducing the number of abortions, even though, as in the case of Planned Parenthood, most of them defend the right to abort for any reason, however trivial. This fact is an indication of the widespread realization that abortion is undesirable, all other things being equal. However, the devotion of pro-abortionists to

---

[16]*Sex Alphabet* (unpaginated), Planned Parenthood Federation of America, 1973. The same page contains a defense of homosexuality that reads in part: "Being a homosexual does not mean that a man or woman carries out strange practices. For homosexuals, lovemaking is as normal as it is for heterosexuals." Of course, if your primary goal is to reduce the population, homosexuality is as effective as abortion.

other values—whether they be sexual liberty, "the right to my own body," or negative population growth—is so strong that they will overlook what must be the inevitable social consequences of millions of abortions in a few years' time.

The Doctors: "Killing Assistants"?

In 1975, when France passed a law permitting abortion on demand during the first ten weeks of pregnancy, the French government's ostensible goal was to *reduce* the number of abortions. The French law has certain provisions which, if taken seriously, might seem to have that effect:

1. A woman desiring an abortion must request it in writing.

2. She must wait one week. During that time certain steps must be taken. At the end of the week, she must repeat her request.

3. The physician must advise the woman of the dangers she runs, both for her own health and for future prospects of parenthood, and she must sign a form acknowledging that she has been so advised.

4. The physician must give her a packet of information concerning the possibilities of adoption and the welfare services that are available to her and the expected infant.[17]

In addition, the law took steps to prevent the establishment of hospitals or clinics specializing in abortion by requiring that no more than twenty-five percent of a facility's cases be abortion-related. Clearly, the French government did not want to create a class of physicians and "health-care" workers who derive their primary revenue from abortion. But this is precisely what we *have* created in the United States. Again, Dr. Denes's book documents the tremendous profits made by one abortion hospital and its active abortionists during New York's brief heyday as the abortion Mecca of America.[18] What does it do to physicians?

---

[17]*L'Avortement. Histoire d'un débat* (Paris: Flammarion, 1975), pp. 284–291.
[18]Denes, *In Necessity and Sorrow,* pp. 230ff.

There can be no doubt that all physicians trained prior to 1968 or 1969, when the tremendous upsurge in abortions came in, were made to feel that abortion was wrong, just as the Oath of Hippocrates says. In fact, in France and Germany, some of the most vigorous opposition to abortion has come from the doctors themselves. In October, 1973, the *Deutscher Aerztetag* (the German equivalent of the American Medical Association) voted overwhelmingly *against* a liberalization of the German abortion law. Anti-abortion physicians argued, "What is permitted will soon become compulsory."

Indeed, that is what is now happening. "Conscience clauses" supposedly protect doctors and hospital personnel from being forced into doing abortions. The older, more established doctors have little difficulty avoiding abortions if they do not wish to perform them. The situation is a bit different with the support personnel, who have less prestige and clout. And it is particularly bad with interns, residents, and medical students. In many hospitals it is impossible for a young doctor to go into gynecology if he or she is unwilling to perform abortions. Since the number of medical school applicants far exceeds the number of places available, it is easy for admissions committees, consciously or not, to weed out those who have scruples against providing "the full range of medical services," including abortions. As a result, we can depend, within one medical generation, on having only doctors who have broken with the Oath of Hippocrates.

We have seen what the Supreme Court said about that Oath, namely that it did not represent the best thinking of (pagan) antiquity and that it owed its popularity only to the influence of Christianity. Consider what the greatest authority on the Oath, Ludwig Edelstein, wrote in a portion of his little book:

> The Pythagorean god who forbade suicide [and abortion] to men, his creatures, was also the God of the Jews and the Christians. . . . the Hippocratic Oath became the nucleus of all medical ethics. . . . In all countries, in all epochs, in which monotheism, in

its purely religious or its more secularized form, was the accepted creed, the Hippocratic Oath was applauded as the embodiment of truth. Not only Jews and Christians, but the Arabs, the medieval doctors, men of the Renaissance, scholars of the Enlightenment and scientists of the nineteenth century embraced the ideals of the Oath.[19]

When an ancient and honorable profession suddenly cuts itself off from its ethical foundations, trouble can be expected. Remember the warning of nineteenth-century physician Christoph Hufeland: "If the physician presumes to take into consideration in his work whether a life has value or not, the consequences are boundless and the physician becomes the most dangerous man in the state." The late General Thomas A. Lane wrote on his deathbed:

> It should be apparent that a medical profession guided by the Hippocratic Oath can win and deserve the confidence of the people. But what happens when the medical profession abandons that Oath to accept an executioner's role in society? A doctor can kill any adult very simply and quickly by administering certain injections, just as a veterinarian puts a sick dog "to sleep."[20] If doctors conceive that they have a rightful power to kill a sick human just as the veterinarian kills a sick dog, and for similar purposes, the whole mentality of the medical profession is changed. It is no longer exclusively the harbinger of life but is now equally the harbinger of death. A sick person cannot know in which capacity the doctor approaches. The relationship of doctor and patient is fundamentally changed.[21]

General Lane was speaking first of all in the context of abortion. But he was aware of the fact that the abortion mentality

[19]Ludwig Edelstein, "The Hippocratic Oath," *Supplements to the Bulletin of the History of Medicine,* No. 1, ed. Henry E. Sigerist (Baltimore: Johns Hopkins, 1943), p. 64.

[20]The state of Oklahoma recently enacted a law providing for capital punishment by "painless injection."

[21]Thomas A. Lane, "Population and the Crisis of Culture," *Human Life Review,* Vol. 1:3 (Summer, 1975), p. 35.

leads, simply and rather directly, to euthanasia.[22] Perhaps no one has stated the reason for the relationship better than the Supreme Court of West Germany.

> From earliest times, the mission of penal law has been the protection of the elemental values of community life. The fact that the life of every single human belongs among the most important legal values has been developed above. The termination of a pregnancy irrevocably destroys human life that has already come into existence. The termination of pregnancy is an act of killing . . . . The currently customary terminology "termination of pregnancy" cannot obscure this factual situation. No legal regulation can pass over the fact that this deed transgresses against the fundamental immunity and inviolability of human life.[23]

What a contrast between the statements "The termination of a pregnancy irrevocably destroys human life" (West German court) and "We need not resolve the difficult question of when life begins" (the U.S. Supreme Court). And a number of legal and medical authorities have pointed out that inasmuch as there is now a right to abortion in America, the Supreme Court cannot logically condemn "voluntary" euthanasia.[24]

Joseph Fletcher not only admits the connection, but he makes a point of it: "If it can be held in the abortion debate that

---

[22]The late Alan F. Guttmacher, M.D., for a number of years head of the Planned Parenthood Federation and an avid pro-abortionist, became a strong advocate of euthanasia after 1973. Prior to *Roe* v. *Wade,* most pro-abortionists denied any connection between abortion and euthanasia. After their victory in *Roe* v. *Wade,* they did not need to fear to espouse euthanasia. Joseph Fletcher, one of the foremost religious exponents of abortion, was also a consistent advocate of euthanasia even before *Roe* v. *Wade.* For a direct treatment of the relationship between abortion and euthanasia, see Helmut E. Ehrhardt, M.D., Ph.D., "Abortion and Euthanasia: Common Problems," *Human Life Review,* Vol. 1:3 (Summer, 1975).

[23]*Bundesverfassungsgericht,* Urteil vom 25. Februar 1975, i BvF I-6/74, English translation by Harold O. J. Brown in *Human Life Review,* Vol. 1:3 (Summer, 1975), pp. 81–82. Full translation by Robert E. Jonas and John D. Gorby in *The John Marshall Journal of Practice and Procedure,* Vol 9:3 (Spring, 1976), pp. 550ff.

[24]Ehrhardt, "Abortion and Euthanasia," p. 27.

compulsory pregnancy is unjust and that women should be free to control their own bodies *even when others' lives (fetuses') are at stake,* do not the same moral claims apply to control of the lives and bodies of people too [to permit euthanasia, italics mine]?"[25]

How quickly the arguments in favor of abortion lend themselves to the justification of euthanasia! Early in the abortion debate, anti-abortionists pointed out that most of the arguments used to defend abortion would apply with even greater logic to infanticide (especially the argument about the possible deformity of the fetus). Now we see that they can also be used to justify euthanasia. If it is harmful to women and men to hand their developing children over to doctors for "termination," what will it do to physicians—indeed, to the whole medical profession—to learn to earn a living by killing instead of healing?

[25]Joseph Fletcher, "Ethics and Euthanasia," in Dennis J. Horan and David Mall, eds., *Death, Dying and Euthanasia* (Washington: University Publications, 1977), p. 265. Reprinted from *To Live and to Die: When, Why, and How* (New York: Springer-Verlag, 1973).

6

What the Bible Says About Abortion

If thou forbear to deliver them that are drawn unto death, and those that are ready to be slain; if thou sayest, Behold, we knew it not; doth not he that pondereth the heart consider it? And he that keepeth thy soul, doth not he know it? And shall not he render to every man according to his works?

—Proverbs 24:11–12

The Bible does not deal specifically with abortion. For that matter, it does not deal specifically with infanticide, the killing of babies. Nor does it talk about parricide, fratricide, uxoricide (killing of one's wife), nor genocide (the killing of a whole race). Examples of such crimes are mentioned, but not singled out for special treatment. In fact, the Bible does not even discuss suicide (self-killing). There are specific provisions against homicide— the deliberate taking of human life ("killing" or "slaying" is the usual expression).[1] The Bible prohibits the taking of innocent

[1] Not all deliberate killing of human beings is regarded by the Bible as culpable homicide. Capital punishment is commanded; self-defense is permitted. The Bible approves of killing in war under certain circumstances. The biblical commandment prohibits murder—the deliberate, premeditated taking of human life—as well as voluntary manslaughter (deliberate, but not premeditated). Abortion is, as the German court said, a homicidal act (from Latin *homo*, as in *homo sapiens*, "human"; the fetus belongs to *genus homo* and therefore is

118

human life. If the developing fetus is shown to be a human being, then we do not need a specific commandment against feticide (abortion) any more than we need something specific against uxoricide (wife-killing). The general commandment against killing covers both.

It certainly does not justify abortion to say, as the U.S. Supreme Court did, "We need not resolve the difficult question of when life begins." If human life has begun, then abortion is homicide and not permissible. If it has not begun, then abortion is just another medical procedure. Obviously, abortion is traditionally regarded as a form of killing, for it is generally included in criminal codes under "crimes against the person." In fact, this is also where the closest thing to a direct biblical reference to abortion occurs, in the section of Exodus following the Ten Commandments and dealing with specific crimes against individuals (Exod. 21:22–25).

With regard to the morality of killing a developing fetus, it is not enough to say we are not sure it is human. We must be able to say we are sure it is *not* human. If a hunter were to see movement in a bush and shoot at it, it would not be enough for him to say he was *not sure* it was not another hunter. He would have to be able to say he was *sure* it was not. How can we be sure the fetus is not a human being? Clearly we cannot; it is far easier to be sure of the contrary, that it *is*. But the Court's whole argument falls if we are even in legitimate doubt about the matter. The Court legalized an action that has a very good possibility of being the killing of innocent human beings.

What Is a Human Being?

The term "human being" is a philosophical or technical one

---

properly called *homo* or *humanus*, "human"; and *occidere*, "to kill"). We seldom refer to abortion as murder (deliberate, premeditated killing) because of the complicating factors involved, such as the mother's stress. But sometimes it offers a surprisingly close parallel: it can be deliberate and premeditated, and it is always killing a human being.

and does not occur in the usual English translations of the Bible. The Bible talks about "man" and "woman," about "mankind," "children," and "people." It does not define "human being" or "man" as a philosophical text might do. But it does have a clear conception of man and human nature, one that begins in Genesis 1 and is carried through the entire Bible.

Significantly, the Bible does *not* make a principled distinction between the child after birth and in the womb. For example, the same Hebrew word, *yeled,* is used of children generally as well as of the child in the womb in Exodus 21:22. The same Greek word, *brephos,* is used of the young Hebrew children slaughtered at Pharaoh's command in Acts 7:19, and of the unborn "babe" John the Baptist in his mother's womb (Luke 1:41, 44).

How does the Bible define man, or what we call the human being? The first and most important clue is given in Genesis 1:27:

> And God created man in His own image, in the image of God He created him; male and female He created them (NASB).

The Bible clearly teaches that man is different from the animals in two significant ways: he is made (1) in God's image, and (2) by a direct divine act. This contrasts with the animals, which the earth brings forth "after their kind" (Gen. 1:21, 24–25).[2]

A second contrast to the animals is given in the account of God's covenant with Noah, in Genesis 9:3–7, (NASB):

> Every moving thing that is alive shall be food for you; I give all to you, as I gave the green plant.

---

[2]Genesis very explicitly teaches a direct, special divine purpose and act in the creation of man. Whether this can be harmonized with theistic evolution is not the issue here. Although I do not believe the biblical evidence indicates an evolutionary origin of the first human pair, substantial attempts to reconcile evolution with biblical Christianity have been made, always insisting, however, on a special divine purpose and creative act in making man, whether out of an evolution-shaped predecessor or not. See Rachel H. King, *The Creation of Death and Life* (New York: Philosophical Library, 1970).

Only you shall not eat flesh with its life, that is, its blood.

And surely I will require your lifeblood; from every beast I will require it. And from every man, from every man's brother I will require the life of man.

Whoever sheds man's blood, By man his blood shall be shed, For in the image of God He made man.

And as for you, be fruitful and multiply; Populate the earth abundantly and multiply in it.

According to the biblical view, then, man is made in God's image. He has stewardship dominion over the animals and may use them for meat. (Elsewhere in Scripture we learn in greater detail of man's stewardship responsibility for the animals God has entrusted to him.)[3] No animal may kill a man without being killed itself, and if one man slays another, he too shall be killed.[4]

Blood Pollution

Our modern world is very concerned about various kinds of pollution—atmospheric pollution, water pollution, radioactive contamination. Each of these things is serious and represents a betrayal of the stewardship responsibility God has entrusted to us. But there are other kinds of pollution. There is moral pollution, the effects of which pervade our society and about which the Bible also speaks. The most serious form of pollution the Bible knows, however, is blood pollution. The shedding of innocent blood pollutes a land and cries out to God for judgment:

So ye shall not pollute the land wherein ye are: for blood it defileth the land: and the land cannot be cleansed of the blood that is shed therein, but by the blood of him that shed it (Num. 35:33).

---

[3]Although the Bible knows nothing of the kind of ecological religion (I call it "ecosophy") that makes the animals equal to or even superior to man, it does express man's responsibility for the gifts of creation and provides the basis for a sound conservationist spirit in dealing with the environment.

[4]Many scholars see in this Noaic Covenant the basis for capital punishment, which is prescribed in other places in Scripture. However, we may read this passage as a description of what will happen to the murderer, not of what society is commanded by God to do to him.

DEATH BEFORE BIRTH

The Jewish law stated that when the body of someone who has been murdered is found and the murderer is unknown, a heifer shall be sacrificed and the elders of the city must pray to God, declaring their innocence and asking that the innocent blood not be laid to their charge (Deut. 21:1–9).

Ignorance of such things, or pretended ignorance, is no excuse:

> If thou forbear to deliver them that are drawn unto death, and those that are ready to be slain;
> If thou sayest, Behold, we knew it not; doth not he that pondereth the heart consider it? And he that keepeth thy soul, doth not he know it? And shall not he render to every man according to his works (Prov. 24:11–12)?

It is evident that the Bible regards willful killing of innocent human beings as a sacrilege, an offense against the image of God in man. Where such a crime takes place and is not punished, or at least is not confessed with prayer and a sacrifice made for it, God will lay the blame on the whole land. While His judgment may be slow, it is sure. If a nation permits the slaughter of the innocent, it surely will bring God's judgment upon itself. *For Christians to stand idly by while such killings go on, especially in a democratic society where they have a voice in government, is not tolerance; it is complicity.* Germany's Christians did their non-Christian fellow citizens no service by failing to speak out against Hitler's excesses, and the bombs that rained on Germany in the early 1940s fell on Christians as well as non-Christians. Admittedly, it would have been difficult, dangerous, and perhaps ineffective to try to protest in Hitler's dictatorship. But would the results have been worse than what actually happened? It is not difficult nor dangerous to protest in America, but the voices of Christians are just beginning to be raised against the shedding of innocent blood.[5]

---

[5]It is paradoxical that the greatest outpouring of Christian protest on any subject in America has been the protracted protest against the FCC's reported

WHAT THE BIBLE SAYS ABOUT ABORTION

What about the unborn child? Does killing an unborn child constitute the shedding of innocent blood?

Arguments in Favor of Abortion

The rise of Christianity resulted in an immediate and unequivocal condemnation of abortion and the practice almost totally died out. As historian William E. H. Lecky pointed out in *History of European Morals,* from the moment people realized they were dealing with man made in the image of God, abortion was on the way out.[6] The doctrine that man is made in God's image is found in Genesis 1:27. But Genesis 2:7 is a passage that is sometimes used to support the view that human life begins with the first breath:

> And the Lord God formed man of the dust of the ground, and breathed into his nostrils the breath of life; and man became a living soul.

Until the infant breathes, the argument goes, it has not yet become a human being, and hence may legitimately be destroyed. At least three things must be said here.

First, it is not necessarily legitimate to destroy anything that is not human. You may kill your own dog if you wish, but you may not kill it with cruelty. You may *not* kill a bald eagle or even break an eagle's egg, and no one argues that the eagle's egg is a human being. Thus even if Genesis 2:7 proved that the baby is not human until it draws its first breath, that would not necessarily justify killing it.

---

plan to curtail religious broadcasting. Many of those same Christians who wonder about the "separation of church and state" when asked to protest against abortion participated in the FCC letter-writing campaign that brought in over 1 million protest letters. The freedom to use the airwaves for religious programming is a precious freedom and has been greatly blessed by God, but no amount of religious broadcasting will cleanse the land of the pollution of innocent blood.

[6]William E. H. Lecky, *History of European Morals* (New York: Braziller, 1955), pp. 20–24.

Second, if ever there was a religious argument used to justify a piece of legislation, this is it. No scientist would claim that a non-baby five minutes before birth becomes a human being five minutes afterwards. To do so would be absurd. Even if the Bible did teach this, no scientist or lawyer could accept this as a basis for law unless he were willing to agree that biblical principles should be written into the law at the expense of science and reason. To say Genesis 2:7 justifies abortion right up to birth, when science and medicine tell us there is no substantial difference between the late fetus and the newborn baby, is really to make a "particular religious dogma" the basis for law—just what the Supreme Court and the U.S. Commission on Civil Rights said must not be done. Thus, paradoxically, the best argument in favor of abortion on demand, the one that says the fetus is not yet a human being, is drawn from Scripture. But is it drawn legitimately? Clearly not.

Third, Genesis 2:7 deals with a unique situation, one that took place only once in all human history: the creation of the *first man.* Since the creation of Adam, a different method has been in use. If God took inanimate matter and made a man from it, as Genesis 2:7 seems to be saying, then obviously what He created was not a human being until it was given life. But the fetus is not "inanimate matter." It is already alive. And it is already human. To apply Genesis 2:7 to human beings who were carried for nine months in a mother's womb before birth is clearly ridiculous. This argument is seldom used by people who take Scripture seriously.

The Laws Against Violence

There is another text that is sometimes used by Christians to support abortion: Exodus 21:22–25.

> If men strive, and hurt a woman with child, so that her fruit depart from her, and yet no mischief follow: he shall be surely punished, according as the woman's husband will lay upon him; and he shall pay as the judges determine.
> And if any mischief follow, then thou shalt give life for life.

WHAT THE BIBLE SAYS ABOUT ABORTION

Eye for eye, tooth for tooth, hand for hand, foot for foot,
Burning for burning, wound for wound, stripe for stripe.

Many modern versions translate the first verse "so that she has a miscarriage" instead of "so that her fruit depart from her." This translation is questionable. But let us assume for a moment that verse 22 does refer to a miscarriage, that is, to an accident that produces a dead premature child. The act, though unintentional, is still punishable. Some authorities argue that since it is not punishable by death, the fetus must be regarded as property, not as a human being. In the context this is silly. The man who injures a slave so that he dies, but not immediately, will not be punished (v. 21). Surely the Bible does not suppose that the slave who dies at once is human, while the one who lingers is not!

Bruce K. Waltke, one of America's outstanding Old Testament scholars, thinks verse 22 refers to a miscarriage, but points out that it certainly cannot be used to justify abortion. First, the injury is accidental. The woman was not even involved in the struggle. There was no intention to injure her, and certainly not to cause a miscarriage. Second, even though it was unintentional, it was a punishable offense. And finally, as the late Jewish scholar Moses David Umberto Cassuto pointed out, this would have nothing to say about the humanity of the fetus. The argument that since only a fine is required the fetus is less than human is invalid, for under Old Testament law the only offense for which no ransom may be taken is premeditated murder, which this certainly is not.[7]

Cassuto himself translates the text as meaning a premature birth: "But if any mischief happen, that is, if the woman dies or the children die, then you shall give life for life, eye for eye, . . ." This is the more natural translation, preferred by the greatest classical Protestant Old Testament commentators, Carl F. Keil and Franz Delitzsch. John Calvin, in his commentary, is very explicit:

[7]M. D. Umberto Cassuto, *Commentary on Exodus* (Jerusalem: Magnes, 1967), at 21:22.

DEATH BEFORE BIRTH

This passage at first sight is ambiguous, for if the word death ["mischief" in the King James] only applies to the pregnant woman, it would not have been a capital crime to put an end to the fetus, which would be a great absurdity, for the fetus, though enclosed in the womb of its mother, is already a human being, and it is almost a monstrous crime to rob it of the life which it has not yet begun to enjoy. If it seems more horrible to kill a man in his own house than in a field, because a man's house is his place of most secure refuge, it ought surely to be deemed more atrocious to destroy a fetus in the womb before it has come to light.[8]

The most that can be said about Exodus 21:22 is that it does not expressly *prohibit* abortion, but we cannot derive any authority to *perform* abortion from it. We are brought back to the question of whether the unborn child is to be regarded as human. In order to answer this, we have to examine the question of what is meant by God's image in man. If the fetus already possesses God's image, then, as far as Scripture is concerned, he is human.

The meaning of God's image in man is variously defined, but most theologians agree that it is only because he was made in God's image that man can relate to God. God takes some interest in the animals (see Jonah 4:11) but He does not relate to them as he does to human beings. If God relates in a personal way to a human creature, this is evidence that that creature is made in God's image. And it is abundantly evident from Scripture that God relates to us and is personally concerned for us *before* birth.

> For thou has possessed my reins: thou hast covered me in my mother's womb.
> I will praise thee; for I am fearfully and wonderfully made: marvelous are thy works; and that my soul knoweth right well (Ps. 139:13–14).

Concerning the prophet Jeremiah, we learn that God chose him before birth and sanctified him in his mother's womb:

[8]John Calvin, *Commentaries on the Last Four Books of Moses,* Vol. III, trans. Charles William Bingham (Grand Rapids: Eerdmans, n.d.), pp. 41–42.

WHAT THE BIBLE SAYS ABOUT ABORTION

> Before I formed thee in the belly I knew thee; and before thou camest forth out of the womb I santified thee, and I ordained thee a prophet unto the nations (Jer. 1:5).

In the New Testament, the yet unborn John the Baptist recognizes the presence of the yet unborn Jesus in his mother's womb when Mary comes to visit Elizabeth:

> For, lo, as soon as the voice of thy salutation sounded in mine ears, the babe leaped in my womb for joy (Luke 1:44).

The psalmist David recognizes that his identity began with his conception:

> Behold, I was shapen in iniquity; and in sin did my mother conceive me (Ps. 51:5).

In short, there can be no doubt that God clearly says the unborn child is already a human being, made in the image of God and deserving of protection under the law. We have already mentioned Lecky's comments on the totality of the early Christians' opposition to abortion. This unanimity prevailed right up to the present era. The views of Catholics on the subject are well known. But Protestant theologians as well are absolutely clear on this issue. We can consult Karl Barth, who writes:

> The unborn child is from the very first a child. It is still developing and has no independent life. But it is a man and not a thing, nor a mere part of the mother's body. . . . He who destroys germinating life kills a man. . . . The fact that a definite No must be the presupposition of all further discussion cannot be contested, least of all today.[9]

Dietrich Bonhoeffer, the Lutheran theologian who was killed by the Nazis in the final days of World War II for his opposition

---

[9]Barth, *Church Dogmatics,* Vol. III, trans. G. W. Bromiley and T. F. Torrance (Edinburgh: T. & T. Clark, 1961), pp. 415ff.

to Hitler, was equally categorical: "The simple fact is that God intended to create a human being and that this human being has been deliberately deprived of his life. And that is nothing but murder."[10]

Among American theologians, George H. Williams, Hollis Professor of Divinity of Harvard, is president of Americans United for Life. Paul Ramsey of Princeton is among the most eloquent advocates of the right to life, not only for developing fetuses, but for the old, the handicapped, and the defective. Albert Outler of Perkins School of Theology, the senior theologian of Methodism in America, is strongly opposed to abortion, as is Francis Schaeffer, probably the most widely read evangelical theologian in the world today.[11] Billy Graham strongly opposes it and was instrumental in the establishment of the Christian Action Council, the largest Protestant anti-abortion group. Thus the widespread illusion that only Roman Catholics oppose abortion is just that—an illusion. Sometimes it is spread through ignorance, sometimes doubtless through the malice of pro-abortion forces who seek to discredit their opponents rather than their opponents' arguments.

A Touchstone of Christian Obedience?

The early African Christian thinker Tertullian explained the difference between Christian and pagan morality:

> For us murder is once for all forbidden; so even the child in the womb, while yet the mother's blood is being drawn on to form the human being, it is not lawful for us to destroy. To forbid birth is only quicker murder. It makes no difference whether one take away the life once born or destroy it as it comes to birth. He is a man, who is to be a man; the fruit is always present in the seed.[12]

---

[10]Bonhoeffer, *Ethics*, trans. Neville Horton Smith (New York: Macmillan, 1955), p. 131.

[11]Schaeffer's major history of Western civilization, *How Shall We Then Live?* (Old Tappan, N.J.: Revell, 1976), devotes a large section to abortion as a symbol of man's rebellion against God and his moral order. See pp. 218–23.

[12]Tertullian, *Apology*, ix.

WHAT THE BIBLE SAYS ABOUT ABORTION

It is fascinating that this third-century Christian, living centuries before the development of embryology, genetics, and the cracking of the genetic code, correctly anticipated what modern biology now knows: "the fruit is always present in the seed." For Tertullian, as for all other early Christians, abortion was part and parcel of the pagan mentality for which life was cheap and mercy unknown.

His Greek-speaking Christian contemporary, Clement of Alexandria, whose book *The Teacher* is the first major treatise on Christian ethics, wrote of the fact that abortion would not only take life but "destroy human feeling with it."[13] Here too an early Christian gives evidence of prophetic insight: what could be more evident than the fact that wholesale abortion effectively destroys the natural relationships of trust and mutual dependence between mother and child, husband and wife, father and child, grandparents and parents? Clement foresaw it; we are experiencing it.

The increase in abortion, amounting in our own day to nationwide abortion on demand subsidized by the state and promoted by government-subsidized sex education in the public schools, has been possible only as a result of a general abandonment of biblical ethics. What it means was stated clearly by an Italian scholar almost a century ago:

> Abortion, elevated to the degree of a social custom, is in sum nothing but the apparent manifestation of a state of decadence of a people, which has very deep roots and which can only be cured with far-reaching remedies, not with the attempt to suppress the manifestation itself.[14]

Ten years ago, virtually every ethicist in America would probably have agreed with Balestrini. Even the small minority that was pushing for "abortion reform" was doing so on the basis of so-called indications, on a limited basis, and claimed to regard

[13]Clement of Alexandria, *The Teacher*, Book II, Chap. 10.
[14]Raffaelo Balestrini, *Aborto, infanticido ed espositione d'infante* (Torino: Bocca, 1888), p. 141.

abortion only as a last resort, a necessary evil. In fact, most pro-abortionists were surprised and rather taken aback by the Supreme Court's decision in *Roe* v. *Wade*. Our growing acceptance of this decadence is a graphic demonstration of the truth of Alexander Pope's lines:

> Vice is a monster of such frightful mein
> That to be hated needs but to be seen.
> Yet seen too oft, familiar with its face,
> We first endure, then fondle, then embrace.

Have we really learned so much more, in ten short years, than people ever knew before? Or is Balestrini right, and are we witnessing the undeniable manifestation of a state of public decadence?

For centuries, opposition to abortion was a spontaneous, natural attitude for Christians of all denominational and confessional backgrounds. Not until the 1950s, when it was patently evident that liberal Christianity had abandoned its foundations in Scripture and the Christian heritage, did some so-called Christians begin to doubt the wrongness of abortion. And even today, despite widespread disagreement on theological interpretations, it is difficult to find a serious Christian—Protestant or Catholic—of any theological stature who calls abortion good.

The support abortion does receive in some denominations, even though often gained by intra-denominational politics and steamroller tactics, is generally accompanied by an indifference to the authority of the Bible and a repudiation of Christian ethics in other areas as well. There are individual Christians who endorse abortion in the mistaken belief that it is not contrary to the teaching of Scripture. But it is extremely rare for a Christian who is confronted with the specific Bible passages relating to human life and dignity to persist in supporting abortion. When such a one does so, it is almost invariably either by denying the facts ("The fetus isn't human" or "It isn't alive") or by repudiating the authority of the Bible, and sometimes by both. In one congregation where I presented the biblical position on abortion, a woman objected that the fetus is not a human being. When I quoted Jeremiah 1:5 to her, she replied, "That's just Jeremiah's opinion."

A Plea for Biblical Catholicity

Catholicity is the real unity that believers in Jesus Christ experience in adversity in spite of denominational differences. Alexander Solzhenitsyn and others who have written of life in concentration camps have attested the unity that Christians discover in persecution, one that transcends many differences of confessional or denominational doctrine.

During the early centuries of the Christian faith, Christians of every language and geographical location were united in their conviction that man is made in God's image and that abortion is wrong. One of the greatest aids to the formation of a strong alliance is a powerful and dangerous enemy. Christians of all denominations have this kind of enemy in the utilitarian, secularistic militancy that rejects both biblical and pagan medical ethics in its rush to kill the unwanted. Certainly there is room here for the practical catholicity of being fellow soldiers in the struggle against a militantly atheistic spirit that, since it cannot strike God directly, aims its blows at the most defenseless of those who bear God's image: unborn children, the "defective," and the old.

7

Some Questions

Where no oxen are, the crib is clean: but much increase is by the strength of the ox.

—Proverbs 14:4

A number of things should be evident from the preceding chapters:

- We are in the midst of a revolution.
- Like all true revolutions, it is exacting a tremendous toll in blood.
- Unlike most revolutions, it is being imposed by those over us and we are being taxed to pay for it.
- Like most revolutions, it works tremendous hardship on precisely those it claims to benefit—in this case, women.
- Abortion is killing.
- What is killed is a human being.
- Therefore, abortion on demand is a threat to the very existence of society.
- Abortion on demand represents a far-reaching repudiation of biblical and medical ethics.
- Its consequences for our nation and for our social order will be overwhelming.

All these things are rather clear and relatively easy to demonstrate to those who are willing to read history, study the Bible, and think things through to their logical conclusions. If they are

132

not evident to enough Americans today, they will be made plain to all of us tomorrow when the inevitable consequences of our present policies become plain for all to see.

Why then does anyone favor abortion? Why does a writer as sensitive as Magda Denes, whose book is a real cry from the heart, favor abortion and even go on the air to say in effect that it is murder, but necessary murder? Obviously there are some serious reasons.

One underlying reason is population control. This reason is seldom put forward because it is so easy to refute. However, since it is in the back of many people's minds we should point out its defects. It has two major flaws, one of fact and one of logic. First, as far as the United States is concerned, the population explosion is a thing of the past. We are already on the down escalator. If nationwide family planning were to be introduced (as the Canadian Minister of Justice recently proposed for his country), it would make sense economically and sociologically to plan bigger families, not smaller ones, because America's net reproductive rate has already fallen below zero.

Second, even if the population explosion were a genuine consideration in the United States, it would not justify abortion. After all, abortion is killing. If reducing the population is our highest goal, then not only is abortion justified, but many other forms of destruction as well. The speed limit on all highways should be lifted altogether. The government should subsidize chain cigarette smoking. Handguns should be available through the mail, as door prizes, and on a program like food stamps. Obviously these suggestions are ridiculous. But perhaps they do illustrate the fact that *if* population pressure justifies abortion, it also justifies many things that, so far, we are not ready to accept.

Leaving population pressure, let us look at those reasons that seem to play the largest role in pro-abortion arguments. They involve (a) the question of whether the fetus is really human life; (b) the rhetoric of "freedom of choice"; (c) the woman's "right to control her own body"; and (d) the separation of church and state.

133

DEATH BEFORE BIRTH

Is It Really Human Life?

It is puzzling and exasperating that this question continues to be raised in the present state of man's knowledge. We have already mentioned the candid statement of *California Medicine* in the midst of the abortion controversy in that state: "The very considerable semantic gymnastics which are required to rationalize abortion as anything but the taking of human life would be ludicrous if not often put forth under socially impeccable auspices."[1] In other words, the California editorialist knows that abortion is taking human life, but feels it is defensible or necessary. Throughout Magda Denes's book it is apparent that the doctors all know they are killing babies in what she calls "heartrending, ambivalent events of absolute necessity." One million-plus absolute necessities a year in the United States?

Philosophy professor Baruch Brody of Rice University writes:

> In an age where we doubt the justice of capital punishment even for very dangerous criminals, killing a fetus who has not done any harm, to avoid a future problem it may pose, seems totally unjust. There are indeed many social problems that could be erased simply by destroying those persons who constitute or cause them, but that is a solution repugnant to the values of society itself.
>
> In short, then, if the fetus is a human being, the appeal to its being unwanted justifies no abortions.[2]

The fetus *is* a human being. But the seven members of the U.S. Supreme Court fail to recognize this. Physicians like the authors of *California Medicine* and psychologists like Dr. Denes know this full well, but justify abortion on pragmatic, utilitarian, or compassionate grounds. German law calls the fetus *ein menschliches Wesen*, "a human being"; French law calls it *un être humain*, "a human being." Older English law (using, as it often did, expressions borrowed from the French), referred to it as

---

[1]"A New Ethic for Medicine and Society," editorial, *California Medicine*, September, 1970, p. 68.

[2]Baruch Brody, *Abortion and the Sancity of Life: A Philosophical View* (Cambridge: M.I.T. Press, 1975), p. 36–37.

the "child *en ventre sa mère*," "in the belly of its mother." The U.S. Supreme Court feels it "need not decide." There is a terrible intellectual and moral dishonesty here; it may not have been apparent to the justices when the case was being presented, but it certainly must be evident to them now. Yet they persist in acting on the basis of what the rest of the world knows to be fiction, similar to the reasoning which held that the Negro slave or the Nazi *Untermensch* (subhuman, e.g. Jew) is not a human in the full sense of the law.

Of all the arguments used to support abortion, the contention that the fetus is not a human being has to be the most dishonest. No one who studies human development can pretend to be ignorant of the facts. Admittedly, there may be some dispute as to precisely *when* fetal life is "fully human," but everyone *knows* it is a long time before birth, and the Supreme Court permits abortions right up to the moment of birth.[3] To use this argument is really to say that one is not interested in the truth but only in convenience and utility. And that is what the abortion argument is all about. To paraphrase psychiatrist David Allen on the subject, if we accept this line of reasoning, we ourselves had better be very careful not to become inconvenient or lacking in utility.

There is no medical or scientific doubt that the fetus is a human being, with its own individual, totally unique, complete heredity from conception—except in the case of identical twins, when this individuality exists at least from implantation, several days after conception. Ethicists such as Baruch Brody and Daniel Callahan, who speak of the embryo being a human being

[3]In dealing with a viable child (one capable of living outside the womb) in Francis Canavan's words, "the most it [the Supreme Court] would concede was the following: 'If the State is interested in protecting fetal life after viability, it may go so far as to proscribe abortion during that period except when it is necessary to preserve the life or health of the mother.' *But this was not to recognize any inherent right of the child* as against the mother, since the child would be protected only if the state were interested in protecting it [emphasis mine]." Francis Canavan, "The Theory of the Danforth Case," *Human Life Review*, Vol. 2:4 (Fall, 1976), p. 8.

somewhat later, are waiting for brain waves—the evidence of definite brain activity—which appear at the latest in the latter part of the *first* trimester.

But even the appearance of brain waves is but growth in what Dr. Ehrhardt calls "one and the same path of life," beginning at conception. Even were we to concede with Brody that the fetus in its very earliest stages should not be regarded as sufficiently developed human life to require protection, it would be clear that aborting the fetus at any point after its full humanity is developed is an act of homicide, one that should be prohibited by law. (Professor Brody also argues for prohibiting abortions prior to the appearance of brain waves, but not on the grounds that such abortions are clearly homicide.) Even with Brody's narrower definition, we must admit that America witnesses hundreds of thousands of homicides per year, one-third of them paid for by the taxpayers of America.

Freedom of Choice?

Pro-abortion forces do not like to call their opponents "pro-life," but prefer to call them "anti-abortion" or even "anti-choice." They themselves, of course, are not "anti-life" or even "pro-abortion," but "pro-choice." This use of language is both clever and effective. It continues the semantic confusion caused by referring to the developing baby first as a "fetus," then as a "conceptus," "abortus," or "the product of conception."

"Choice" is a good word to Americans. No one wants to be anti-choice. Unfortunately, "choice" in itself is an empty word. To be allowed to choose is not necessarily good; to be forbidden free choice is not necessarily bad. *It depends on the context and the content of the choice.*

At one time the state of Utah allowed a condemned criminal to choose between death by hanging and death by the firing squad. This was "freedom of choice." But neither can be called a very desirable option. Freedom of choice is not very good when both alternatives are undesirable. "Freedom of choice" is not what we want when we are ignorant of the nature of the things between which we are choosing; if offered a choice between two apparently identical glasses, one of which contained pure grape juice, the other grape juice with cyanide, it would be more important to know which is which than merely to have "freedom to choose."

"Choice," like many other words such as "faith," "sincerity," and "commitment," is an empty word apart from its content. We do not expect, nor will the government permit "freedom of choice" where primary principles of law are concerned. We have no "freedom of choice" about killing a person who has offended us, even though some people may sincerely believe that according to their traditional ideas of honor they are obliged to avenge certain insults with death.

We do not have "freedom of choice" where secondary principles are concerned, such as the payment of taxes. No one could argue successfully "I believe in freedom of choice, and this year I choose not to pay." In fact, we do not even have "freedom of choice" where relatively minor, tertiary principles are concerned. If stopped for traveling seventy miles per hour, a motorist will not get much consideration by arguing he should have freedom of choice.

Freedom of choice is therefore meaningless as an argument in the abortion situation. Since abortion is taking a human life, then freedom of choice is no more of a justification for it than it would be for killing one's spouse in order to be able to freely choose another. If abortion were not taking a human life, then there would be no need to defend it. It would simply come within the sphere of normal exercise of ordinary rights.

It is interesting that in modern America we are to be denied "freedom of choice" even with respect to a relatively innocuous substance such as saccharin. It is apparently not good for rats in immense doses, and therefore, for our own good, we are not to have it. The manufacturer who continues to make it after an FDA ban goes into effect can be sure he will not escape penalties just by arguing he wants to give customers freedom of choice.

DEATH BEFORE BIRTH

It is significant that this argument of freedom of choice plays no role in the serious legal discussion of abortion. But it does play a role in popular debate, particularly in the media. Therefore it must be analyzed and seen to be what it really is—a slogan without content. "Having faith" may sound like a generally good idea, but the value of faith depends on its content and its object. Having faith in Satan, as certain cultists do, is quite a different thing morally, intellectually, and practically from having faith in Christ.

A Right to My Own Body?

Here again we are confronted with a slogan that begs the principal question. In general, we have the right to control our own bodies. But this control must stop when we use our bodies to injure another. A man's right to control his own body does not entitle him to get his exercise by beating up someone else or by raping a woman. Clearly, our right to determine what we do with our bodies does not give us the right to injure another.

The case of the pregnant woman is a special case. In almost no situation other than pregnancy is the life of one human being totally dependent on another. The developing child makes constant demands on his mother. (Of course, he will make them even more stridently after birth. But after birth someone else can meet those demands; before birth, only the woman who is carrying him can.) These demands constitute an imposition, one that deprives the woman of certain possibilities of self-development and causes her some physical exertion and distress. But does she have the right to relieve herself of these demands at the cost of another's life? Clearly not; for if she did, she would appear also to have this right after birth when the child's demands are even greater.

The pregnant woman who does not want her child has no greater *physical* burdens placed on her than the pregnant woman who does want him. The demands the child makes do

138

not in themselves determine the woman's reaction to her pregnancy. Her reaction may be one of serious mental and emotional distress. It may be compounded by various complicating factors: the reaction of her husband, her boyfriend, her parents, and others. But all these things, serious though they may be, cannot justify the destruction of another human life, particularly when it could be saved by simply waiting out the pregnancy and then giving the child up for adoption. If such considerations are taken as the justification for destroying unborn life, then there is no reason in principle why they should not also justify the taking of life after birth.

The right to control one's own body, like all other rights, involves a measure of responsibility. Prior to sexual intercourse (except in the case of rape) the woman has the right to refuse intercourse. If intercourse is going to take place, the woman has the option of contraception (as does the man). But if conception has occurred, a new human being has been brought onto the scene and the woman's right has run up against a new responsibility. What our laws should do—as the laws of Sweden provide—is to make sure the man *shares* the woman's responsibility. The way to equality must be the equalization of responsibility, not equal denial of responsibility.

The Separation of Church and State

The so-called "First Amendment" argument did not figure prominently in the Court's reasoning in *Roe* v. *Wade*, inasmuch as the Court claimed that it "need not decide" when life begins. It was present only by implication in the assertion that the Hippocratic belief that life begins at conception was based on "dogma" and that the state of Texas was espousing "one theory of life" (by implication a religious one) in forbidding abortion except to save the life of the mother.

However, once anti-abortion sentiment burst over the heads of the authors and defenders of *Roe* v. *Wade*, the "separation of church and state" argument was trotted onto the field. Perhaps the best example of this is the Report of the Civil Rights Commission:

> So long as the question of when life begins is a matter of religious controversy and no choice can be rationalized on a purely secular premise [false, as indicated above!], the people, by outlawing abortion through the amending process, would be establishing one religious view and thus inhibiting the free exercise of religion of others.[4]

Yet, strangely, the Civil Rights Commission *defends* the government's right to prohibit polygamy, which the Mormons claimed to be part of the exercise of their religion.[5] Why? In its original form, the Mormon religion *commanded* polygamy. No religion *commands* abortion; it is more than a bit peculiar to speak of the performance of abortion as "the free exercise of religion." Furthermore, it can at least be argued that polygamy does not injure anyone, and that it involves only consenting adults. (The same misleading arguments are made in favor of the toleration of homosexual behavior!) Abortion usually involves two "consenting adults," the woman and the doctor, although sometimes the woman more or less has the abortion forced on her and often the doctor is acting, if not under duress, at least under some pressure. Operating room personnel, too, may not be "consenting." But there is one party to the abortion—the developing child—who certainly is neither an adult nor consenting.

The Civil Rights Commission justifies its support for the laws against polygamy while bitterly opposing any restrictions on abortion, on the theory that to oppose abortion is to stand for a particular religious dogma. (There is, of course, a latent anti-Catholicism in this polemic against "religious dogma." Now that

[4]U.S. Commission on Civil Rights, *Constitutional Aspects of the Right to Limit Childbearing* (Washington, 1975), p. 31.
[5]*Ibid.*, pp. 37ff.

most expressions of racial and religious prejudice are in such great disfavor, attacks on Roman Catholics for their opposition to abortion remains one of the few socially acceptable expressions of bigotry practiced today.) The theory that opposition to abortion necessarily rests on a "religious" (for "religious," read "Catholic") dogma is absurd. Non-Christians ranging from the pagan "Father of Medicine," Hippocrates, to the contemporary Jewish philosopher, Baruch Brody, oppose abortion on the basis of nothing more "religious" or "dogmatic" than their knowledge of the fact that the developing fetus is in fact a human being.

But even if the view that the developing human life is fully human were of exclusively religious origin, writing laws to protect such life would not "establish a religion" any more than prohibiting bestiality (sexual relations with animals) establishes Judaism.

Let us look a little more closely at this repeated appeal to the First Amendment. It reads, in part: *Congress shall make no law respecting an establishment of religion, or prohibiting the free exercise thereof.* The first part of the amendment guarantees the freedom of the press. Why is there this interesting combination of "freedom of the press" with the so-called "separation of church and state"? To answer the question, let us see what the so-called "establishment clause" actually means.

Congress is not to establish a national church. This is precisely what the First Amendment says and means. At the time it was written, it did not even forbid the establishment of state churches. In fact, state churches existed in Connecticut and Massachusetts, the "cradle of liberty," until well into the following century. Later the Fourteenth Amendment extended to the individual state legislatures the limits set upon the powers of Congress in the First Amendment. Since that time, it has been unconstitutional for a state to establish a state church.

Is the protection of developing life "an establishment of religion"? Clearly it is not, any more than the laws against other forms of homicide represent an establishment of religion. If the argument of the Civil Rights Commission were valid and no laws could be passed except for wholly secular reasons, then we would also have to drop the laws against murder, assault, rape, and similar crimes. There are practical secular reasons for forbidding such behavior, but the reasons are not "wholly secular." Certainly the laws against murder, for example, historically came into being as religious sanctions.

It was God who told the Hebrews that their laws, for example against killing members of their own nation, must also apply to "the stranger that sojourneth with you" (Num. 15:16). Secular self-interest and group solidarity tells us we must stand by others who resemble us; it took the law of God to tell us we must also protect the stranger. If the Civil Rights Commission had said we may have no laws for which there are *only* religious reasons, that would be more reasonable. But it is next to impossible to write a sensible law for which there is only a "wholly secular" justification and no religious one. In the case of laws against abortion, there *are* secular justifications, just as there are for laws against adult homicide. Professor Brody's book, *Abortion and the Sanctity of Life,* written from a wholly secular viewpoint, is a compelling argument.

Strictly speaking, the First Amendment does not mandate the "separation of church and state," although Thomas Jefferson interpreted it in this way. It certainly does not mandate *total* separation, which in any ultimate sense is impossible. Even if religion is shoved back to what former Associate Justice Tom C. Clark called "the inviolable citadel of the human heart and mind," it will soon find itself in conflict with the state even there. One example is the government-funded propagation of a kind of sex education that in effect legitimizes homosexuality (as discussed in chapter 5). If selling homosexuality isn't an assault on the "inviolable citadel," it is hard to imagine what would be. Inculcation in witchcraft? (Apparently that too happens in government-funded schools.)

Freedom of the Press + Freedom of Religion = ?

We can understand the original goal of the establishment clause best if we notice that it is in the same context with protection of the freedom of the press. Clearly the intent of the two clauses was to guarantee that the government not control the minds and consciences of the citizens. It was not to control their thinking by telling them what to read. It was not to control their worship by establishing a church.

The First Amendment prohibits the state from dictating to the conscience of its citizens. It does *not* prohibit the conscience of the citizens from speaking to the state. If we understand the First Amendment correctly, we will recognize that far from telling us that those of us who have religious convictions may not speak to the state, it is intended to *protect* our consciences so we will be able to speak to the state. If Christians may not bear witness to the state of standards of right and wrong as they see them because those standards have a religious origin, then there will be no standards in America, a country founded on Christian principles.

Using the First Amendment argument to preserve the "constitutional right" to abortion on demand is an absurdity. But because it is a popular absurdity, we need to be prepared to point out two things. First, opposition to abortion is based on very valid secular reasons as well as on religious ones. Second, the First Amendment does not bar the conscience of citizens from speaking to the state; this would be the end of meaningful democracy.

Summary

The most frequently voiced pro-abortion arguments are based on fallacies, specifically on the allegation that the unborn child is not human life. This is precisely what the U.S. Supreme Court refused to decide, although it effectively treated it as nonhuman. If this issue is squarely faced, it becomes apparent that the other arguments in favor of abortion are ruses, irrelevant, or inapplicable. It is precisely this issue that pro-abortionists do not want to face, for if they do—as even pro-abortion Civil Rights Commission chairman Arthur Flemming admits—they will have to legislate to protect that human life.

It is for this reason that programs not at all related to the abortion question, such as the French film *The First Days of Life,* are frequently kept out of the very schools that distribute Planned Parenthood's "Sex Alphabet." The junior-high or high-school student who sees *The First Days of Life* will understand something of what killing a developing child means and will not be so susceptible to the argument that abortion for "medical or personal reasons" is quite the thing to do.

Almost four years have passed since *Roe* v. *Wade.* President Ford appointed a new associate justice to the bench, but he voted with the pro-abortion majority in *Danforth.* The Court has had plenty of time to reflect on the enormity of its errors in *Roe* v. *Wade.* In several recent decisions, it has refused to expand *Roe* v. *Wade* to include an *obligation* of the government to fund abortions, but it continues to defend its earlier decisions permitting abortion on demand. These 1977 decisions in no way limit the freedom to abort nor do they forbid the use of tax money to fund abortions. They only state that such funding is not a constitutional right.

It is apparent that we cannot rely on the present Supreme Court to undo the wrong it has done. If citizens recognize the evil of abortion on demand and understand that as voters in America they are responsible for the laws of this country, they have no alternative but to attempt to reverse the Court. The only apparent means to this end is a constitutional amendment.

8

Death by Pragmatism

O ye hypocrites, ye can discern the face of the sky; but can ye not discern the signs of the times?

—Matthew 16:3

In the last analysis, the argument for abortion boils down to this: the end justifies the means. Joseph Fletcher, who is so ardently pro-abortion that it seems impossible to him that anyone could be against it, clearly admits this: "The crucial question is not whether the end justifies the means (what else could?) but *what justifies the end?*"[1] What justifies the means (any means, including the elimination of all defectives and "worthless" life) is what he calls the *summum bonum* (Latin, "highest good"), namely human "happiness." Happiness for Fletcher seems to involve a combination of physical well-being and personality development.

Once we accept Fletcher's basic principle, we are on the way to seeing humanity, in Muggeridge's words, "as a factory-farm whose primary consideration must be the physical well-being of the livestock and the material well-being of the collectivity." According to the Westminster Catechism, which in this case represents the view of all the major Christian communions, the chief end of man is "to glorify God and to enjoy Him forever." To reduce man's chief end to "happiness" in Fletcher's limited

[1]Joseph Fletcher, "Ethics and Euthanasia," *To Live and to Die: When, Why and How* (New York: Springer-Verlag, 1973), p. 119.

145

sense is a proposal that few American politicians would espouse. But it is an end to which seven American so-called justices have committed our whole nation.

Abortion on demand is based on the argument that the end justifies the means. It assumes, of course, that the end is a good one. But in the case of the abortion argument, our nation has never officially committed itself in any way to the idea that that particular end is good: population control, negative population growth, relieving people of the responsibility of childbearing and child care at any cost. If we really believe this end is desirable, we had better be careful. There are many other means that serve it even better than abortion.

While he was still alive, Mao Tse-tung was frequently reported to have been willing to gamble on a nuclear war, reasoning that at least 200 million Chinese would survive, enough to control the world after the annihilation of most of the population of the other superpowers. That is "negative population growth" with a vengeance. But if human life has no positive, intrinsic value, then nuclear war is a valid means to the end. Indeed, sudden death in an atomic holocaust is no doubt less traumatic than death by saline abortion or starvation.

Most Americans do not like to think in terms of presuppositions (the assumptions underlying a particular position) nor of consequences (the long-range results a particular course will bring). We are "pragmatists" and proud of it. If a thing works, we want it. Pragmatism has its merits within certain limits, and those limits involve an understanding of values. The supersonic transport certainly "works." America, however, decided it wasn't worth the cost in money and in the damage to the environment, and so canceled work on the Boeing SST. But where there is no agreement about values, pragmatism can sweep everything aside.

Make no mistake: the fundamental argument for abortion on demand is pragmatic—it works. The end justifies the means. And the end is utilitarian: the greatest good for the greatest number. In any abortion decision those who will profit from the abortion outnumber the one who will be hurt. The woman will profit, or at least thinks she will; otherwise she would not seek the abortion. The doctor will profit because he has Medicaid, backed by HEW and the United States taxpayer, to guarantee his bill.[2] And there are a few others who have a stake in it too: the man, perhaps; other hospital workers; and perhaps even HEW itself, which can add to its staff for purposes of "Abortion Surveillance" and other abortion-related activities. The fetus never belongs to the "greatest number."

In the long run, we believe, everyone will suffer from mass abortion and its consequences. But at the moment it seems to be for the "greatest good of the greatest number" to permit and even to subsidize the destruction of those little ones. There is an old Latin legal maxim, *De minimis non curat lex:* "The law is not concerned with trifles." But the Latin can also be translated, "The law is not concerned with the littlest ones." In this translation it would be a good motto for the U.S. Supreme Court, to go right under the present phrase, "Equal Justice Under Law."

The pro-abortion argument, although often couched in compassionate terms, is essentially a utilitarian argument. Indeed, the "compassionate" angle is highly overworked. As Brody points out, if abortion is indeed killing, there is nothing particularly noble about refraining from having an abortion. It is only what should be expected. Nor can it be genuine "compassion" to ease the predicament one person must suffer at the price of destroying another—especially when that other could be saved at the cost not of life, but only of several months inconvenience and perhaps some embarrassment and social discrimination.[3]

Brody goes so far as to say what this writer would not: that the pregnant woman who does not have an abortion has no particular claim on the support and encouragement of society. Admittedly, refraining from a crime—whether the murder of an adult

---

[2]In federal district court hearings Aug. 3, 1977 in New York, Planned Parenthood Federation produced testimony from a number of abortion clinics to the effect that no abortions would be performed unless payment is guaranteed. So much for the abortionists' "compassion" for women in distress.

[3]Baruch Brody, *Abortion and the Sanctity of Life: A Philosophical View* (Cambridge: M.I.T. Press, 1975).

or a fetus—is not in itself a virtuous deed deserving of reward. But when we recognize that in general no woman desires an abortion in itself, but only for the purpose of being relieved of the burden she finds hard or apparently impossible to bear, it is only reasonable for society to help her bear it.

The U.S. Supreme Court would never admit to making utilitarianism its *summum bonum*. No senator, representative, or president could be elected on a utilitarian platform. As a matter of fact, in the 1976 election candidate Carter made a point of his idealism, not of his utilitarianism. And certainly people would not have voted for a candidate with the slogan, "The end justifies the means." But the slogans people use are less important than the way they act. In the case of abortion, the underlying principle is clearly that of utilitarianism—and short-range utilitarianism at that—for we have no assurance that the "greatest number" that thinks it benefits from abortion today will not find it suffers from the consequences of abortion tomorrow.

Abortion is not a medical problem except in very rare cases. It is a moral problem in the sense that it involves a choice and a decision of the will: a choice to reject the developing child and a decision of the will to "terminate" it. Abortion also is not "a medical act," in the words of an outstanding French medical authority. It is certainly not a medical act in the traditional sense of the word, for it destroys life rather than enhancing it. Even if we admit loose language and call abortion a medical act because it is performed by medical personnel, we have no reason to expect "medical acts" to be the long-range solution for moral and spiritual problems. If we accept the principle of medical "solutions," then of course we are on the way to many other things: control of "deviant" behavior (including, just possibly, religious faith) by psychosurgery, behavior modification by drugs, and government imposition of the values it thinks appropriate to the kind of society it wants.[4]

---

[4]For a fuller discussion of this issue, see my recent book, *The Restitution of the Republic* (New Rochelle: Arlington, 1977).

DEATH BY PRAGMATISM

Both "the end justifies the means" and "the greatest good for the greatest number" are thoroughly bad principles, if taken as ultimate principles. On an intermediate level they have some value provided that limits are set. It is precisely this question of limits that the Court and American society as a whole have evaded in the abortion issue. If this is where we are now, where do we go from here? The abortion revolution leads to the "Brave New World."

A Valid Principle

There was a period, not all that long ago, when it was customary in America to speak of the "infinite value" of every human life. That may have involved some exaggeration, especially as it was generally meant in a humanistic, man-centered way, without reference to God. It led to strenuous efforts in the medical field, particularly in the 1950s and 1960s, to preserve the last spark of life as long as possible, no matter what the cost to the individual, his family, and society. It was almost as though the medical profession as a whole had lost all consciousness of its limited power and no longer saw itself as a helper in life, but almost as a creator.

By the late 1960s, and now with a vengeance in the 1970s, a terrible reaction seems to have set in. It is almost as though the medical profession is saying, "Since we cannot prevent death, let us take the responsibility for it. Let us impose it." The logical result of such a development is euthanasia—and not only in the desperate, aggravated, protracted cases that are always brought up in discussion—but for everyone, when the "greatest number" shall decide that "capability of meaningful life" is at an end.

For the exaggerated humanistic principle of the "infinite value" of each human life, Christians can and should substitute a conviction of the absolute dignity and worth of each life, not because of its "quality of life," whether that be seen in terms of physique, health, mental ability, or any other human measure, but because man is made in the image of God. Indeed, even the "defective" are God's handiwork. He told Moses: "Who hath made man's mouth? or who maketh the dumb, or deaf, or the seeing, or the blind? have not I, the Lord?" (Exod. 4:11).

The "Sanctity" of Life

We are accustomed to speaking of the "sacredness" or "sanctity" of life. It is precisely this "sanctity" which is attacked by the Supreme Court decision and in consequence by everyday American practice. Knowing that "sanctity" comes from *sanctus*, "holy," many Christians are uncomfortable with the term "sanctity of life." We know that human life is not "holy" per se in the sense of possessing an innate holiness.

But "holy" has another, more valid sense. It is in this sense that all Christians are called "saints" (also from Latin *sanctus*). To be holy means to be "separated unto the Lord," reserved for God's special purpose. It is in this sense that we can properly speak about the sanctity of human life. It is for this reason that the shedding of human blood was forbidden to both man and animals and could be done only on the basis of an explicit divine commandment. Although "sanctity" sounds like a religious term, Christians should feel no more embarrassment in calling on our highest court to recognize the sanctity of life than does Watergate special prosecutor Cox, in the passage cited in chapter 4:

> Oddly, but possibly because counsel did not stress the point, the opinion [*Roe* v. *Wade*] fails even to consider what I would consider to be the most compelling interest of the State in prohibiting abortion; the interest in maintaining that respect for the paramount sanctity of human life which has always been at the centre of Western civilization, not merely by guarding "life" itself, however defined, but by safeguarding the penumbra [surrounding shadow], whether at the beginning, through some overwhelming disability of mind or body, or at death.[5]

[5]Archibald Cox, *The Role of the Supreme Court in American Government* (New York: Oxford, 1976), p. 52.

DEATH BY PRAGMATISM

If the United States will not safeguard the sanctity of life (and that is just what our government, through the Supreme Court, has now attacked) we can understand Cox to be implying that it is attacking the center of Western civilization. America learned to respect and trust Archibald Cox for his integrity and judgment in the Watergate affair. Should we blithely disregard his judgment here?

Neither law professor Cox nor philosophy professor Brody make any special point of a religious basis for their commitment to the sanctity of life. Yet each of them has taken the trouble to protest, in the painstaking, exact way of scholars, what appears to them to be an atrocity. Those of us who are Christians understand that we have a solid, even irrevocable commitment to the sanctity of life. The issues of life and death are reserved for God and we may not assume His prerogative by deciding which life is "meaningless" and ready for destruction. Can Christians, in obedience to God, do less than secular scholars for the defense of what God has reserved for Himself, the "issues of life"?

Jesus reproached the Pharisees, the religious experts of His day, because they could not "discern the signs of the times." What will be the defense of today's Christians, if it should turn out that it is the secular scholars, not we, who discerned the signs of our times seven years before *Nineteen Eighty-Four*?[6]

---

[6]While this manuscript was in press, the United States Supreme Court ruled that neither the state governments, nor by implication the federal government, are *required* to pay for abortions for indigent women. This is certainly a step in the right direction, but it falls far short of *protecting* developing life. It merely provides the *possibility* that citizens not be obliged to pay for destroying it (June 22, 1977). President Carter and the House of Representatives have come out squarely against federal funding of elective abortions and the Senate has espoused the same principle, although with loopholes. These are all very praiseworthy developments, but they should not lead to complacency as long as *Roe* v. *Wade* still determines the fate of hundreds of thousands, even millions, of unborn infants.

9

The Road Ahead

I recognize full well the chance for errors in judgment. Because of that I try to err only on the side of life.

—C. Everett Koop, in *The Right to Live; The Right to Die*

According to the familiar hymn, there is no sorrow that heaven cannot heal. That is true, but not all sorrow has to wait for heaven for healing. In human society there is much sorrow that can be helped or even healed on a personal or group level. There is some that requires legal or government action. A personal injury requires a personal act of restitution or atonement; a governmental injury requires a governmental act to make it good.

Abortion as we know it in America involves both personal and governmental injuries. There is much that can be done about it on the personal level, and those things we should do, as individuals and as members of Christian congregations, on our own responsibility. But there are some things that require government action to repair the wrong it has caused and to avert wrong in the future.

Personal Action

Perhaps much that is in this book comes as a surprise to the reader. Most Christian readers will proabbly be surprised not by the major positions taken here, but rather by the extent of the damage that has already been done and by the massiveness of the threat to the future of American society. If anything is surprising—and by no means the whole story has been told in these pages—then my first challenge to the reader is this: Get the facts! Inform yourself!

Information

The first task facing a Christian who is in any sense disturbed, challenged, or unsettled by the abortion situation as pictured here is to get the facts. A number of books have been cited. Reading many books is not everyone's hobby, but if a reader has come to this point, he will certainly be ready for the next one: *The Right to Live: The Right to Die* by Philadelphia surgeon C. Everett Koop.[1]

One of the most important things to do is to understand the facts about human development. Somehow in all the enthusiasm for sex education, down to the details of sex technique, we have overlooked one of the major things sex is all about— where babies come from! Here there is no better visual aid than the French film already mentioned, *The First Days of Life*. The film, which is available from many local right-to-life groups,[2] has nothing to do with abortion. But viewers will quickly understand what the victim of an abortion is: a tiny, developing human being. A great variety of literature and visual aids is available; a partial list is included as Appendix A.

Motivation

The second stage of the task, after information, is motivation. For the individual who wants to obey the principles of God's Word, information will provide its own motivation. It is at this point, when personally motivated to act, that an individual Christian must seek to involve others. The same procedure of

---

[1] *The Right to Live: The Right to Die* (Wheaton: Tyndale, 1976).
[2] In case of difficulty, information can be supplied by the Christian Action Council, 788 National Press Building, Washington, D.C. 20045.

providing information—medical, legal, and biblical—undertaken and outlined in this book will apply to the congregation or local fellowship group. Once a congregation has been informed and motivated, it will naturally proceed to implementation.

Implementation

Implementation will require action on the two levels mentioned: on the personal, voluntary, congregational, or fellowship level and on the governmental level. Let's look first at the voluntary level.

We have spoken many times of the little victims of abortion—the unwanted babies who are destroyed. But we should never lose sight of the fact that in almost every case, the woman or young girl involved is also a victim. She may have something on her conscience and if she proceeds with an abortion she will carry a load of guilt in the future; but at the moment she is a victim. Whether married or unmarried, she has been exploited by a man. Together they have created a situation that God meant to be a shared responsibility. She has been left, or sent, to face it alone. In the case of a married couple considering an abortion, determining the task of pastor, congregation, and fellow Christians is fairly simple. Except in those very rare cases where there are genuine medical indications for an abortion, there is hardly a family in wealthy America that cannot surmount in some other way the problems an abortion is supposed to solve.

Where there is a real economic problem, there are so many ways to cope that it is primarily a question of finding them and being willing to use them. Indeed, if there really are too many children, there is nothing wrong with a family giving up a child for adoption. True, when father and mother are living together, intra-family adoptions are more common than the use of an adoption service. But where an intra-family adoption does not seem wise, Christian parents who genuinely seem unable to cope with another child should be encouraged to consult a reliable Christian family service organization.

Certainly pastors and friends should avoid giving the impression that giving one's child up is shameful. In circumstances where it seems impossible or extremely difficult to care for a new child, giving it up may seem an error. But as Dr. Koop points out, it is better to err in the direction of life than in that of death. These issues must be brought out into the open and discussed; there is many a Christian family today that has the destruction of a developing child on its conscience because the parents felt that the course of giving him up for adoption would not be understood. An abortion they could keep quiet; a birth and adoption would quickly become known and talked about.

What is true in the case of a Christian married woman seeking an abortion is also true in the case of the Christian unmarried woman. She has problems—more problems than the married woman, for she has been involved in personal sin—but there are better ways to deal with those problems than by abortion. Nothing is more natural than sexual relations, and nothing is more natural than for them to produce a child. Although sex outside of marriage in unlawful in God's sight, it represents, to use C. S. Lewis's terminology, an abuse of love. Destruction of the child that results from such unlawful love is no longer love. It is selfishness. And though born out of desperation and often easy to understand, if not to condone, it can never be blessed.

There are a number of problems in the way sex is handled in schools and in the general media, on the one hand, and among Christians on the other. The general media approach to sex is almost always one of technique: how to have intercourse, how to prevent conception, how to have an abortion. The general Christian approach, at least to the unmarried, is almost always one of morals: how to avoid sin. We who are Christians ought to know better because each of us is himself a sinner, but we often give the impression not only that sin ought to be avoided, but that it *will* be—and that if it isn't, we don't want to hear about it. There needs to be a realistic approach to the consequences of out-of-marriage sex among Christians, particularly among young people. Pregnancy is avoidable, but that doesn't make sex outside of marriage all right. Birth is also avoidable through abortion, but that doesn't make abortion all right.

All teaching on sexuality should include two elements: (1) the responsibility of boys and men, first of all towards girls and women, and secondly towards the children they beget; and (2) the responsibility of girls and women towards a child they may conceive, even out of wedlock.

A Christian girl who is pregnant out of wedlock does not need to be taught shame, which really has no place in the Christian life. She is probably full of shame already. She needs to hear the gospel message of 1 John 2:1-2: "If anyone sins, we have an Advocate with the Father, Jesus Christ the righteous; and He Himself is the propitiation for our sins; and not for ours only, but also for those of the whole world." Sin is sin, but when it is confessed it can be completely and eternally forgiven. And she also needs to know that her family, her Christian friends, and her congregation will stand by her in her decision to allow the baby to be born and to care for it, whether in her own home or by giving it to a responsible service agency for adoption.

Legal Remedies

Christians, if they take the steps indicated above, need not fear they are contributing to pressure on girls and women to seek abortions. They may have confidence that through their encouragement, prayer, and practical support they are helping some babies to be born rather than aborted. But such personal steps and local congregational measures will do nothing to rid us of the guilt we involve ourselves in as a nation by permitting mass nationwide abortion to continue.

The Supreme Court, as Professor Steamer indicated, has placed us in a situation in which the only way out is what he calls the "unlikely" route of a constitutional amendment. But we Americans have amended our Constitution quite a few times;

recently we guaranteed eighteen-year-olds the right to vote. If that was worth a constitutional amendment, can we say that protecting lives is not? Senator Birch Bayh (D.-Ind.), who in his capacity as chairman of the Subcommittee on Constitutional Amendments, Senate Judiciary Committee, bottled up the anti-abortion amendments late in 1975, told many anti-abortionists that amending the Constitution is a serious business, not to be engaged in for petty causes. At present, he is sponsoring an amendment to insure the direct election of the president.

Are we to accept the judgment that direct election of the president (which only once in our history would have produced a different result than the present electoral college system) is more important than the lives of millions of unborn Americans? Whatever the ultimate fate of the Equal Rights Amendment, can anyone reasonably say that the rights it would secure to women (a subject much in dispute, we acknowledge) can possibly be more important than the right to life, which America currently denies to one in four unborn children?

David Louisell, late professor of constitutional law at the University of California, described *Roe* v. *Wade* as a "perfect challenge" to America's Christians. If we will not react to the substitution of ancient religion—the standards of Roman paganism—for biblical values, to being obliged to help fund the extermination of one-quarter of the future generation, then we will probably react to nothing. And as though *Roe* v. *Wade* were not enough, the Court increased the provocation in *Planned Parenthood* v. *Danforth*. Apparently the Court and much of the government are confident that America's Christians are what Mao Tse-tung called the United States—a paper tiger, hollow and without teeth.

We Christians often feel sorry for ourselves in a "secular, pluralistic" society. But we should be careful. God can read the U.S. Constitution too. He too knows what it is in our power to do. He too is fully aware that under the principles of American democracy the people are *expected* to act to remedy evils, not to wait supinely for the remedies to be handed down from above. This is what self-government is all about. And by a kind of irony of history, we seem to be in a position where Christians are faced with the choice between getting serious about the responsibilities of self-government or becoming serious candidates for self-destruction. "If thou sayest, Behold, we knew it not; doth not he that pondereth the heart consider it? And he that keepeth thy soul, doth not he know it? And shall not he render to every man according to his works?" (Prov. 24:12).

10

The Watchman

And if it is disagreeable in your sight to serve the Lord, choose for yourselves today whom you will serve.

— Joshua 24:15, NASB

What is the Christian's calling in today's world? Clearly it is to be a witness. When the Lord Jesus was about to be taken up into heaven, He told His disciples: "You shall be my witnesses both in Jerusalem, and in all Judea and Samaria, and even to the remotest part of the earth" (Acts 1:8, NASB). The Greek word for witness is *martys*; the witness's testimony is his *martyrion*. From these words we derive our English "martyr" and "martyrdom." A principle part of the witness Christ requires of us may be designated as martyr-witness.

The original connotation of *martyrion* is a testimony before authorities; the witness, on the demand of the authorities, tells what he has seen and heard. This is precisely what Peter and John do in Acts 4:20. It is that of which Jesus spoke: "When they deliver you up, do not become anxious about how or what you will speak; for it shall be given you in that hour what you are to speak" (Matt. 10:19, NASB). In this original connotation, *martyrion* did not imply suffering nor *martys* dying for one's faith. They came to have those meanings because one who gave a consistent *martyrion* before the pagan authorities frequently suffered or even died for it.

We are still called upon to give a testimony for the Lord and sometimes even to bear a witness of the *martyrion* type. In religiously free America we seldom have to fear retaliation for bearing witness to Jesus Christ, particularly if we couch it in terms of *our personal faith.* After all, if belief is a private and personal matter, who can criticize us for what we believe?

We must be careful here, however. There is more to a testimony than just a report of one's own faith. The witness or testimony is to be of Jesus Christ and His gospel, not simply of our own personal experiences and feelings. And when we bear witness to the fulness of God's Word, we may begin to say disagreeable things that result in the suffering aspect of *martyrion,* which in English we call martyrdom.

John the Baptist told Herod, "It is not lawful for thee to have her [Herodias]" (Matt. 14:4). This resulted first in his imprisonment and later in his execution. John was a martyr in the common sense of the word, but not in precisely the sense Jesus meant in Acts 1:8. He died for his testimony, but it was not, at least not in the strict sense, a witness to Jesus. What kind of testimony was it?

It may be helpful to distinguish between "martyr-witness" and "watchman-witness." By the first we mean witness to Jesus Christ, perhaps before the authorities, whether or not it results in suffering. By the second we mean a warning testimony to the law of God and to the judgment we incur when we break it.

It is often customary to distinguish between "preaching the gospel" and "moralizing." Indeed, there is a sense in which moralizing is far removed from preaching the gospel. However, according to Luther's famous maxim, there are two parts to the gospel—law and gospel. It is important to know which is called for at any particular time. Luther's maxim was: "Preach the law to the proud, the gospel to the brokenhearted." And clearly the law of God has the function of bringing an awareness of one's condition, a sense of sin, and of one's need for a savior. Thus Paul calls it "our schoolmaster to bring us unto Christ" (Gal. 3:24). Preaching the law of God may correspond to what Paul means by "the whole counsel of God" (Acts 20:27).

THE WATCHMAN

Watchman-Witness

This second category of witnessing, watchman-witness, is not optional. It is part of the "total package." One of the things of which we must beware in speaking to congregations or even to individuals about abortion is the possibility of preaching the law to the brokenhearted. Despite the claims of some pro-abortionist women who say in effect, "I have had an abortion and I'm proud of it," I venture to say there is not one woman who has had an abortion, not even for the very rare medical necessity in which her own survival was involved, who is not in some sense brokenhearted over it. The vehemence with which militant pro-abortionists justify their positions testifies to heartbreak, or at least to heartrending, as Magda Denes calls it.

When dealing with any group in which there may be people who have been involved in abortion, a Christian should be careful to include full references to the gospel promise of forgiveness of sins and of new life in Christ. These promises apply whether the abortion was secured prior to conversion or as a Christian. Unfortunately, the case against abortion is so strong that discussing it often comes through to those who have been involved as a terrible condemnation. This, coupled with the sorrow and remorse they almost inevitably already feel, makes preaching of the law a burden that is almost impossible to bear.

Yet many of those in the pro-abortion camp are proud. Anyone who has heard Associate Justice Blackmun defend his position on abortion can hardly avoid the impression of a terrible arrogance. It would be wrong to attribute arrogance to another individual, for only God knows the heart. Yet when one encounters persistent and determined adherence to a fundamentally wrong position, one may charitably think that it is caused by "invincible ignorance." Having said this, it would be less than charity to fail to declare to a person holding such a position that it involves a transgression of the law of God, and that he must beware lest he have no answer when called to give an account for his soul.

DEATH BEFORE BIRTH

The model for the watchman-witness, the testimony that declares the law as well as the gospel, particularly to the proud who are secure in their self-righteousness, is found in Ezekiel:

> Son of man, I have made thee a watchman unto the house of Israel: therefore hear the word at my mouth, and give them warning from me.
>
> When I say unto the wicked, Thou shalt surely die; and thou givest him not warning, nor speakest to warn the wicked from his wicked way, to save his life; the same wicked man shall die in his iniquity; but his blood will I require at thine hand.
>
> Yet if thou warn the wicked, and he turn not from his wickedness, nor from his wicked way, he shall die in his iniquity; but thou hast delivered thy soul . . . (Ezek. 3:17–19).

The prophet Ezekiel receives this calling because the Word of the Lord came expressly to him (Ezek. 3:3). What is a Christian today? Is he not one who has heard the message of salvation according to the Word of God and trusted in Jesus Christ for salvation, according to the Word? Can there be a Christian to whom the Word of God has *not* come? If not, can there be a Christian who is not, at least to some extent, given the task of being a watchman as well as a martyr?

It is no good to argue at this point that Israel was a theocracy and that God's Word was also civil law. In Ezekiel's time, the Israelites were exiles in Babylon, not only under foreign domination but in a territory where the state cult was the worship of Marduk, not the God of Abraham. Ezekiel had no power to *enforce* his warnings. In that respect, we in America, in a nation with a largely Christian tradition and with democratic institutions, are in quite a different situation. If even Ezekiel, to whom the Word of the Lord came, was to admonish and warn the wicked (and also the righteous—see 3:20–21), what about us in modern America?

The answer seems obvious: it is our responsibility to warn our fellow Christians and our fellow Americans of the danger of death that comes with transgression of God's moral law. If they will not hear, that is *their* responsibility. If we fail to tell them, it is *ours*.

We are, according to Romans 13, to be obedient to the civil authorities, and the duty of these authorities is to reward good and punish evil (Rom. 13:3–4). But in the United States, we the people are the authority. Therefore it is we, not a king or emperor, who will have to answer to God for the justice of our institutions.

As we have seen, there is no pollution that is worse than the pollution of innocent blood. Nazi Germany unleashed a world war and persecuted the Jews. Christians in Germany had very little to say about Hitler's policies, at least after he was in power, but the bombs fell on Christians as well as on secular Germans and committed Nazis. To the extent that there was a religious opposition to Hitler, it was the Catholics who were prominent. And it was the Catholic parts of Germany that fared comparatively better in the disaster that befell that nation. Catholic Bavaria and the Rhineland are free. Protestant Prussia, so long the stronghold of a kind of orthodoxy, has disappeared from the map. Is there any lesson to be drawn from this for America's Protestants, who are by and large leaving the watchman-witness against abortion to the Roman Catholics?

No other country in the Western world has as large a percentage of churchgoing and supposedly committed Christians as the United States. And certainly no other major country has a chief of state who so openly proclaims himself a Bible-believing Christian. Would it not be a travesty for the United States to continue as the only country in the world, Christian or non-Christian, that not only legalizes but subsidizes the slaughter of the innocent, not only early in pregnancy but right up to the moment of birth? Does not a Christian president deserve the testimony of Christian people, reminding him of the demands, promises, and warnings of God's Word? "[If] thou givest him not warning, nor speakest to warn the wicked from his wicked way, to save his life; the same wicked man shall die in his iniquity; but his blood will I require at thine hand" (Ezek. 3:18).

DEATH BEFORE BIRTH

American Christians are, for the most part, prepared to pay the price in taxes for the shedding of blood. Even the President and the Secretary of Health, Education, and Welfare, both of whom have denounced abortion, seem forced to tolerate it and to go on paying for it despite their immense powers of action and persuasion to change the situation. At this writing, a determined group of effectively pro-abortion senators, including such unexpected figures as Edward Kennedy (D.-Mass.) and Robert Byrd (D.-W.Va.) seem determined to override the reluctance of the House of Representatives and the President and to force all America to keep on paying the abortion bills.[1] We can pay the medical bills for all the abortions Americans want; they are, after all, only a small portion of the Gross National Product. But there is another reckoning to give: will we be able to settle it? "His blood will I require at thine hand."

[1]Senator Robert Byrd, the majority leader, told me on September 8, 1977, that he is "against abortion." On September 9 he stepped down from the powerful Conference Committee and passed over two anti-abortion Democrats—Stennis and McClellan—to name pro-abortion Senator Inouye (D.—Hawaii) to replace him.

Appendix

ABORTION, INFANT DEATH, AND CHILD ABUSE

Year	1973	1974	1975	1974–1975 % change
Total Reported Abortions*	763,500	900,000	1,100,000	+22.2%
Infant Deaths (under one year)	56,000	52,400	50,700	− 3.4%
Child Abuse Cases Reported	n.a.	229,400	294,800	+19.8%
Child Abuse Cases Investigated	n.a.	147,100	233,700	+58.6%
Child Abuse Cases Verified**	n.a.	88,100	139,300	+57.3%

Figures supplied by the National Child Abuse Center, Denver, Colorado.

---

*Figures for 1974 and 1975 are estimates. The totals of reported abortions each year 1969–1972 were 22,670 in 1969, 193,500 in 1970 (first year of New York's liberalized abortion practices), 485,500 in 1971, and 586,500 in 1972. By 1973 *Roe* v. *Wade* had legalized abortion on demand nationwide. It is widely held that even these reported totals, high though they are, do not include nearly all the legal abortions as many jurisdictions and facilities do not report fully. It has also been widely held that *prior* to legalization, the number of abortions actually performed — mostly illegal — greatly exceeded the reported total of less than 23,000 reported in 1969, for example. However, these repeated claims of a very high number of illegal abortions prior to 1970 in New York and prior to 1973 nationwide cannot be substantiated by any correspondingly high figures for maternal death due to consequences of illegal abortion. In addition, the drastic drop in the number of babies available for adoption after 1970 would make it apparent that far more unwanted babies were aborted legally after 1970 than had ever been aborted illegally prior to that year.

**Because the collection and tabulation of figures for child abuse is only just beginning on a broad, systematic basis, the very high increases from 1974 to 1975 probably reflect improvement in reporting as well as increase in child abuse. However, it is evident that the decline in the number of unwanted babies through abortion is not accompanied by any apparent decline in child abuse.

Bibliography

The literature on the topic is vast. Here are mentioned only a few particularly significant works, many of them especially valuable from the Christian perspective.

Bajema, Clifford. *Abortion and the Meaning of Personhood.* Grand Rapids: Baker, 1974. A solid treatment by a theologian in the Calvinist tradition.

Brody, Baruch, *Abortion and the Sanctity of life.* Cambridge: M.I.T. Press, 1975. A philosophical inquiry by a Jewish scholar who began as a pro-abortionist but was led by his research to the opposite conclusion.

Denes, Magda. *In Necessity and Sorrow.* New York: Basic Books, 1976. Ostensibly "pro-abortion," this book by a New York City clinical psychologist documents the reality of abortion for the women, the physicians, the other health care personnel, and the victims.

Human Life Review (quarterly). Published at 150 East 35th Street, New York, N.Y., 10016. The outstanding scholarly periodical in the field, furnishes indispensable material on abortion and related topics, such as euthanasia, fetal research, and genetic engineering.

Koop, Everett. *The Right to Live/The Right to Die.* Wheaton: Tyndale, 1976. An outstanding Christian surgeon discusses abortion and euthanasia from both medical and biblical perspectives.

Noonan, John T., Jr. *A Private Choice. Abortion in America in the Seventies.* New York: Free Press, 1979. The most up-to-date legal presentation of the pro-life position.

Wertham, Frederick. *A Sign for Cain.* New York: Macmillan, 1966. Deals with medical ethics in the Third Reich.

Wilke, Dr. and Mrs. J. C. *Handbook on Abortion.* Cincinnati: Hiltz, 1971. A valuable, straightforward, illustrated discussion of the ugly reality of abortion by two outstanding pro-life activists.

Index

INDEX